W9-ACX-980

THE GRATEFUL DEAD

★ ★ ★ ★ ★ ★ ★ ★ ★ ★ ★ ★ ★ ★ ★

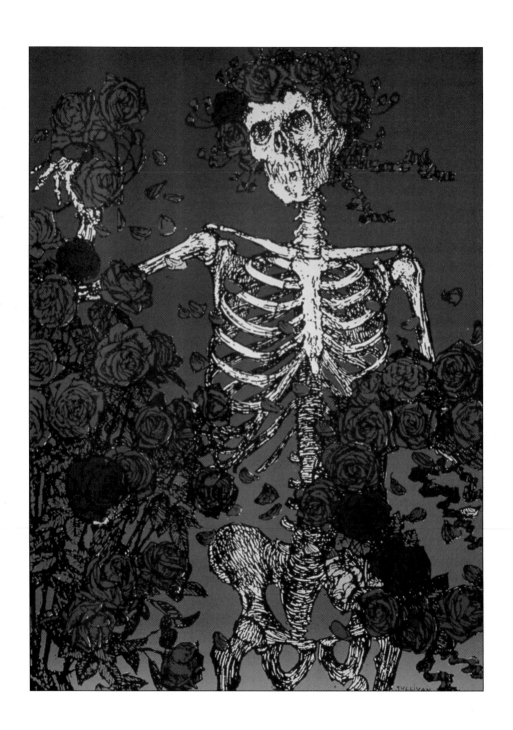

POP CULTURE LEGENDS

THE GRATEFUL DEAD

★ ★

SEAN PICCOLI

CHELSEA HOUSE PUBLISHERS

★ Philadelphia ★

CHELSEA HOUSE PUBLISHERS

EDITORIAL DIRECTOR Rick Rennert
PICTURE EDITOR Judy Hasday
ART DIRECTOR Sara Davis
PRODUCTION MANAGER Pamela Loos

Staff for THE GRATEFUL DEAD
ASSOCIATE EDITOR Therese De Angelis
EDITORIAL ASSISTANT Kristine Brennan
DESIGNER Alison Burnside
PICTURE RESEARCHER Patricia Burns
ORIGINAL COVER ILLUSTRATION BY Stanley Mouse ©1996

3 5 7 9 8 6 4

Library of Congress Cataloging-in-Publication Data

Piccoli, Sean.
The Grateful Dead / Sean Piccoli.
          128 pp. cm.—(Pop culture legends)
Includes bibliographical references and index.
Summary: Portrays the popular touring band the Grateful Dead, led by
Jerry Garcia, who achieved a devoted following of Deadheads and
gained fame for their lengthy, improvisational songs.
ISBN 0-7910-3250-7
      0-7910-4454-8 (pbk.)
1. Grateful Dead (Musical group)—Juvenile literature. 2. Rock musi-
cians—United States—Biography—Juvenile literature.
[1. Grateful Dead (Musical group) 2. Musicians. 3. Rock music.]
I. Title. II. Series.
ML3930.G735P53   1997   96-39425
782.42166'092—dc21   CIP
[B]   AC MN

FRONTIS:
The 1966 poster that introduced artist Stanley Mouse's
classic skull and roses design for the Grateful Dead.

Contents ★ ★ ★ ★ ★ ★ ★ ★ ★ ★ ★ ★ ★ ★ ★ ★ ★ ★

A Reflection of Ourselves

Leeza Gibbons

I ENJOY A RARE PERSPECTIVE on the entertainment industry. From my viewpoint, I can see the sizzle and excitement of popular culture. By nature or design, pop icons generate interest because they mirror our society.

Who are your heroes and heroines? Who do you most admire? To whom do you look for inspiration and guidance? What type of person would you like to be? How do we decide who are the most popular and influential members of our society?

According to recent polls, you will probably respond very differently than your parents or grandparents might have at your age. Surveys determining who young people most respect and admire have shown that entertainers, athletes, and popular artists are increasingly replacing world leaders. In the past 15 years, for example, General Norman Schwarzkopf was the only world leader chosen as the number-one hero among high school students. Other names on the list include Michael Jordan, Eddie Murphy, Burt Reynolds, and Sylvester Stallone.

In the 1960s, Pop artist Andy Warhol predicted that one day every American would be famous for 15 minutes. It may be easier today to achieve that fame, but it is also much harder to keep it. Reputations can be ruined as quickly as they are made. Yet some artists and performers continue to inspire and instruct us, despite changes in world events or popular tastes.

Why do some artists remain fascinating, while others are quickly forgotten? What qualities give them such power over our lives? The artists and entertainers profiled in this series often have little more in common than the enormous influence that each of them exerts on the popular imagination.

Some offer us an escape: actress Marilyn Monroe, comedian Groucho Marx, and writer Stephen King have used glamour, humor, and fantasy to distract us from everyday life. Others present all too recognizable images: folk singer Bob Dylan's uncompromising realism challenges us to confront what disturbs us. Some offer us reassurance: animator Walt Disney provides us with a sense of security and continuity. Others shake us up: composer John Lennon and actor James Dean continue to inspire fans to reevaluate the world.

Pop culture legends react to fame in diverse ways. Singers Michael Jackson and Prince carefully guard their personal lives from public view, while others, like Madonna, enjoy putting their private lives before the public eye.

But all of these artists and entertainers share the rare ability to capture and hold the public's imagination in a culture that thrives on novelty and change. The books in this series examine the lives and careers of these legends and the society that values their work. Each volume presents a man or woman whose extraordinary talent, stubborn commitment, and great personal sacrifice has produced work of enduring quality and influence in today's world.

As you read these books, ask yourself the following questions: How are the careers of these individuals shaped by society? How do these people help to shape the world? What captivates us about their lives, their work, or the images they present? By studying the lives and achievements of pop culture legends, we may ultimately learn more about ourselves.

★ ★

POP CULTURE IMAGES:
THE ART OF STANLEY MOUSE

THE WORK OF STANLEY MOUSE is as unique as the musicians for whom he created the distinctive skull and roses design. Like the Grateful Dead, Mouse came of age in the "San Francisco scene" of the 1960s, the era of the hippie and of Haight-Ashbury, of Victorian architecture and tie-dyed T-shirts, of Acid Tests and weekend music festivals.

Originally a custom-car detailer, Mouse became a "hot rod artist" whose airbrushed, pop-eyed monster cartoons adorned thousands of T-shirts on the American car-show circuit. In 1959, he established a mail-order business called Mouse Studios and a retail shop called The Mouse House, with a staff that included his parents and two artist assistants.

After studying painting and life drawing at the Art School of the Society of Arts and Crafts in Detroit, Mouse migrated to San Francisco with a caravan of friends who called themselves the Laughing Academy. There, he met Alton Kelley, a fellow hot-rod artist and a partner in the Family Dog entertainment troupe, which staged dance-hall events in the Bay area.

Kelley's connection landed Mouse a job creating promotional posters for Family Dog. Soon the two were collaborating—Kelley coming up with the ideas and Mouse executing the designs. Family Dog's reputation for eccentricity allowed Mouse and Kelley to experiment broadly with composition, lettering, and imagery. Their work evolved into a characteristic style, filled with visual puns that captured the playful, anything-goes spirit of Haight-Ashbury. During this period, the duo created their first poster for the Grateful Dead—misspelling it as "Greatfull"—and came up with one of the most widely recognized images in rock and roll, the skull and roses motif.

Stanley Mouse and Alton Kelley remained associated until 1980, when Mouse relocated to Santa Fe, New Mexico, to concentrate on his

8

own painting and drawing. After that first Grateful Dead handbill appeared in 1967, Mouse Studios designed concert posters for the Jefferson Airplane, Big Brother and the Holding Company, Cream, the Rolling Stones, and Paul McCartney and created signature images for Journey (a winged scarab) and the Steve Miller Band (Pegasus). Mouse continued to be the Grateful Dead's premier graphic artist, turning out posters, album covers, and T-shirts, including the famous Rainbow Foot and Ice Cream Kid designs for the Dead's 1972 European tour.

More recently, Stanley Mouse has concentrated on the more traditional arts of painting and drawing. Still, he says, people seem to "prefer the flashy art of my past." As a visual historian of rock music, Mouse has truly earned a place among pop culture legends.

Broken Arrow

CHOP!

Clifford Garcia swung the axe forward, splitting the chunk of firewood just as little brother Jerome pulled back his hand. The halves fell away and Jerry hoisted a fresh log for his brother Clifford to chop. Jerry steadied the wood with his fingers, then yanked his hand clear of the blade—*chop!*—with inches to spare. The two smiled at one another.

It was a dare that Clifford—"Tiff"—and Jerry played on family camping trips. The Garcias—José, a Spanish-born musician and bar owner, his wife, Ruth, and their two sons—were in the Santa Cruz Mountains south of San Francisco on a summer weekend in 1947. The Garcias entrusted the job of collecting and cutting firewood to the boys. They could hear them laughing as they worked. Chop! Giggling voices drifted through the trees. *Chop!*

Suddenly, Jerry was screaming.

The wood was split, but part of Jerry's finger was gone. Ruth Garcia frantically bundled the boy's hand in a towel and José drove his son to a hospital, where the wound was treated.

Later, when the bandages were removed, four-year-old Jerome Garcia,

A high school dropout and failed U.S. Army soldier, Jerry Garcia, shown here in 1968 before a San Francisco crowd, nevertheless transformed the Grateful Dead from a locally based bluegrass band into one of the most popular and successful rock bands in America.

11

a dark-haired boy with deep brown eyes, would be forever different from other kids. He had lost half of his right middle finger.

He might have given his entire hand, though, to prevent what happened a year later. In the spring of 1948, José was fly-fishing in deep water when he lost his footing; the strong current seized him and pulled him down. Jerry was playing on a nearby bank and saw his father go under.

Ruth Garcia was left alone with two children to raise and a waterfront hotel and bar to run. It was more than she could handle. So she sent Jerry to live with his maternal grandparents in a working-class neighborhood a few miles from their home in San Francisco's Excelsior district. For the next five years, Ruth's parents would raise Jerry. The boy would visit his mother's tavern, the Four Hundred Club, and listen to sailors tell their travel stories at the bar.

In 1952, Jerry returned to live with his mother, who had remarried. At 10 years old, Jerry was now nearly a teenager—and a handful for his mother and stepfather. He had developed a willful streak and a smart mouth while living with his grandparents. And later at Denman Junior High, he began keeping company with kids who carried razors for self-protection.

Denman's student body was divided into warring camps: the Barts (shorthand for "Black Barts," or the "greasers" from the city's blue-collar neighborhoods) and the Shoes (mostly upper-middle-class kids named for their fashionable white shoes). Membership in one of these cliques was a means of surviving in an environment where fights erupted easily and often and spilled over into weekends. Shoes and Barts would troll each other's neighborhoods looking for fights and settling scores with fists, boards, and razor blades.

And every gang member was a target. As a Bart, Jerry often came home with a split lip or with bruises and gashes from run-ins with the Shoes. More than once, he was hurt badly enough to go to nearby Mission Emergency Hospital.

Finally, Jerry's mother, fearing for her son's safety, again moved out of the city, into the suburb of Cazadero, where Jerry began attending Analy High School in Sebastopol, a 30-mile bus ride from Cazadero. He hated every day of it.

Jerry was bored by classroom subjects and instead read authors whose books were not found in public-school libraries: the philosophers Arthur Schopenhauer, Martin Heidegger, and Immanuel Kant, among others. He took art classes on weekends—a practice that would have shocked his former Bart buddies—and developed a strong interest in music.

As a teenager in the 1950s, Jerry was fascinated by the irresistible new sound of rock and roll and listened endlessly to guitarists like Chuck Berry, Gene Vincent, Buddy Holly, Eddie Cochran, and Bo Diddley (shown here). Of the guitar, he later said, "It was all I wanted to play."

Jerry's childhood had been steeped in music. His father was a bandleader, proficient with several instruments, who had performed for a living before the Great Depression. José Garcia had even named his younger son after his favorite composer, Jerome Kern, who created such classic Broadway musicals as *Show Boat* and *Roberta*. Jerry's brother, Tiff, liked "doo-wop" acts like the Crows and the rhythm and blues of Hank Ballard and the Midnighters. His grandmother loved to listen to radio broadcasts from the Grand Ole Opry in faraway Nashville, Tennessee, America's country music capital. One of Jerry's own favorites was bluegrass vocalist and mandolin player Bill Monroe, whom he heard while living with his grandparents.

Then there was the piano. Though his mother insisted that Jerry take lessons, he never learned to sight-read. He faked his way through eight years. "Music was something I was not good at," Garcia would recall years later in an interview with *Rolling Stone* magazine. "I was attracted to music very early on, but it never occurred to me it was something to do [for a living]."

Sometime in the mid-1950s, Jerry heard rock and roll for the first time. Performers like Bill Haley and the Comets and Elvis Presley delighted the teenager with their rocking, rolling, howling rhythmic style, a revved-up hybrid of rockabilly, blues, and country. Like the wildest horse or the fastest car, rock and roll demanded your attention. It was dangerous, delirious, and irresistible. Jerry fell "madly in love" with it, listening most closely to rock and roll guitarists Chuck Berry, Gene Vincent, Buddy Holly, Bo Diddley, and Eddie Cochran.

Whatever style of music Jerry listened to, all of his favorite artists had one thing in common—the guitar. "That's what I wanted to play," Jerry said simply. He asked his mother to buy him one. Remembering his stubbornness with piano lessons, Ruth Garcia balked. Jerry pleaded; he wanted a guitar. Finally, his mother met him halfway: she brought home an accordion for his 15th birthday.

Jerry was so dismayed that finally his mother relented. She traded the old Neapolitan accordion for a cheap electric guitar—a Danelectro, a popular starter brand—and a baby Fender amplifier, from the same company that built Buddy Holly's guitar. All Jerry had to do now was learn how to play.

Surprisingly, missing the top half of a finger on his picking and strumming hand caused Jerry no trouble at all. More vexing was his inability to tune the guitar properly to the musical notes E, A, D, G, B, and E—from the lowest to the highest string—standard tuning for most guitarists. "Then I met a guy in school who showed me the right way to tune it," he said, "and four chords, maybe five chords—the basic first-position chords and stuff. I had to unlearn somewhere between six months and a year's worth of self-teaching."

Jerry's immediate attraction to rock and roll did not seem to be shared by many others. The sound was still new and exotic and only Garcia and a few of his pals listened to it. Even the members of his first band, a five-piece combo of Analy High School kids, wanted to play mellow saxophone songs, while Jerry longed to play guitar like Chuck Berry or Gene Vincent.

By the 1950s, San Francisco had become a busy cultural center, fed in part by the influence of numerous area colleges and universities. In search of new musical experiences, Garcia took to hanging around coffee houses to hear folk musicians and local poets, who generally despised rock and roll and listened almost exclusively to jazz.

Folk lyrics of the period reflected the irony of the American condition—the extremes of wealth and poverty in the prosperous, post-World War II age of beloved war hero and president Dwight D. Eisenhower. The so-called "Beat poets" of the '50s, who sprang from the counterculture crowd known as the beatniks, drank coffee as black as their turtlenecks and railed in verse against the one-house-two-kids-and-a-car life that defined the American Dream.

The beatniks did not go to church on Sundays; they did not vote Republican; and they did not attend PTA meetings, as they believed all of "straight" America did. Instead, they immersed themselves in the dark, self-absorbed writings of long-dead French poets like Arthur Rimbaud and Charles-Pierre Baudelaire.

The Beats also used sex and drugs to experience extremes of pleasure and distress. But they did not consider their experimentation a game. College educated and compulsively literate, the Beats viewed such conduct as research and expressed their "findings" in their own poetry and fiction. Beat writers like Allen

Beat poet Allen Ginsberg leads a group of demonstrators in New York City's Greenwich Village in protesting a marijuana prohibition. Beatniks experimented widely with legal and illegal drugs in an effort to break the rules of conventional society and achieve altered states of mind.

Ginsberg, Lawrence Ferlinghetti, and Michael McClure taunted "straight" Americans, daring them to live as they did.

Along with Ginsberg's ranting, sexually charged poem "The Howl," the work of fiction that best defines the Beat generation is writer-wanderer Jack Kerouac's novel *On The Road*. The book traces the physical and spiritual adventures of fast-talking Dean Moriarty as he travels across America. Moriarty savors the essence of experience, of living moment to moment and daring anything, despite hunger, solitude, and poverty. All you need, Kerouac says, is the right attitude. And maybe a car.

Dean Moriarty is a marauding loner with a last-chance view of life that threatened the way in which Americans during the 1950s viewed the world. The book moved Jerry Garcia even more than did the wild stories of the sailors in his mother's tavern. The young guitarist found in the novel a model for living.

But Jerry was not Dean Moriarty, and Analy High had no room for such a character. He began skipping school, sneaking rides into San Francisco to run with the same kids his mother had tried to keep him from years earlier. He started smoking marijuana—a common Beatnik practice—and often stole his mother's car to visit girlfriends.

In his junior year, Jerry dropped out of high school altogether. At 17, his scrapes with the law were routine. He was running out of options. Jerry's endless legal and academic problems led him to an institution that knew exactly what to do with troublemakers: the United States Army. He enlisted in 1959, with his mother's blessing, and was sent to Fort Ord, California, for basic training. The army hammered into Jerry the virtues of discipline, order, and obedience. It was like taking piano lessons all over again.

After boot camp, Jerry was assigned to Fort Winfield Scott in San Francisco, where he received missile training and was given motor pool and administrative duties. But soon he started skipping roll calls and going AWOL (absent without leave). He was court-martialed twice before finally receiving the military's harshest sentence short of imprisonment: a dishonorable discharge.

Garcia's army career lasted nine months. He was 18 years old and it was 1960. He was a high-school dropout and a failed U.S. soldier whose strongest interest was in his Sears Silvertone guitar.

2 Friends of the Devil

OR THREE YEARS AFTER HIS ARMY DISCHARGE, Jerry drifted around the peninsula, living in apartments, group houses, and sometimes cars, while attending art school and practicing music. Though he showed great promise as a visual artist, music was his first interest. He formed groups with names like the "Sleepy Hollow Hog Stompers," the "Hart Valley Drifters," the "Thunder Mountain Tub Thumpers," and the "Wildwood Boys," performing with various band members both on live radio broadcasts and in stage competitions. His music, a mixture of folk, jug, bluegrass, mountain, and rag, included tunes like "I Was Born in East Virginia," "Long Black Veil," and "Matty Groves."

Garcia had developed a following in the Bay Area and was a busy but still-struggling musician when he met Sarah Ruppenthal, a Stanford University film student and musician. The two began dating; soon after, they were performing around Palo Alto, California, as the folk duo "Sarah and Jerry." They married in May of 1963, when Ruppenthal was three months pregnant, and their child Heather was born that December. At 21, Garcia was now a husband and father—and he needed a full-time job.

The Warlocks in 1965. From left: Jerry Garcia, Bill Kreutzmann (drummer), Bob Weir (guitarist), Phil Lesh (bass), and Ron "Pigpen" McKernan (guitarist).

In December of 1963, Jerry Garcia walked into Dana Morgan's Music Store in Palo Alto and offered his services as a guitar teacher. The guitars, drums, and keyboards occupying nearly all of the floor space at Morgan's represented only one part of the shop's business. Owner Dana Morgan, Sr., also paid several music teachers to give lessons for many of the instruments he sold. The store was a meeting place as well for scores of working and aspiring musicians in and around the peninsula town, where Stanford University was situated.

With the folk music movement in full stride and rock and roll growing more popular, the demand for guitar lessons was increasing. "Every damn fool had to have a guitar and walk around strumming it," Morgan said. "But Garcia didn't look like a fool. He was a very immaculate, tall, thin boy. He had coal-black hair and a little mustache. He looked like a Spanish gentleman." Morgan hired him on the spot.

At Dana Morgan's, Garcia began playing another stringed instrument—the banjo. The bluegrass music he had heard as a child while listening to Grand Ole Opry broadcasts with his grandmother affected him strongly. "That banjo just . . . it just made me crazy," he said. Soon Garcia was an accomplished bluegrass instrumentalist— in a community of jazz and folk musicians.

Playing bluegrass demands nimble hands and an ear for intricate melody, and Garcia mostly taught himself how to play it. He set aside his electric guitar to concentrate on acoustic guitar and banjo and developed into a pure "picker," an adept finger stylist.

But even in San Francisco, this down-home country sound had an audience. Bluegrass is an honest, pure, stark kind of music. Its lyrics commonly speak of love and death, of work and drink, of God and the coarse southeastern country landscape. For Garcia, the music contained a basic truth. Eventually, he combined the traditional area folk sound with bluegrass and captivat-

ed many of the intellectuals and students in coffee houses and art galleries around the peninsula, where he had
begun performing on his five-string banjo and six- and
twelve-string guitars.

Garcia was waiting for his students while strum-
ming his banjo one evening in the shop when Bob
Weir, a high school student from the upscale suburb of
Atherton, California, walked in.

Bob was not looking for lessons; he already played
guitar. In fact, he was teaching younger kids at Dana
Morgan's—when he wasn't sweeping the floors there.
Hearing banjo music from the street, he and a friend
came in and told Garcia to forget about seeing his students that evening. "It was New Year's Eve," Weir
recalled. "He was absolutely unmindful of the fact . . . so
we acquainted him with that information."

But that wasn't the end of their encounter. Garcia
had keys to the front of the shop where the new instruments were kept, recalled Weir,

> so we talked him into breaking in . . . and we grabbed
> a couple of guitars—the ones we'd always wanted to
> play. He had a good time playing and singing and
> kicking stuff around all night, and by the end of the
> evening—I don't know what time it was—we decid-
> ed we had enough second-rate talent to throw togeth-
> er a jug band.

Garcia recognized Weir's skills as more than second-
rate. A slim kid with straight hair and almost girlish
good looks, Weir was too young to be served in some of
the bars and taverns where a band would play. He had
discovered the Beatnik scene in the same way as
Garcia—by hanging around coffee houses and watching
musicians for style points.

Weir's father was a mechanical engineer and his
mother a direct descendant of the *Mayflower* Pilgrims.
Weir had grown up in upscale Atherton with all the

advantages of a wealthy family. But he had been expelled from seven different prep schools for offenses ranging from disrespect toward teachers to flinging himself off the school roof for kicks.

Bob excelled in sports, especially in football and track. He was bright and talkative, and when he wanted to, he earned perfect grades. But he was more interested in chasing girls and having fun—and prep schools provided him with opportunities for both, to the chagrin of his teachers and parents.

Bob also had a problem that doubled his difficulties at school. He had dyslexia—a neurological disturbance that impairs one's ability to read. (Though medical researchers have since learned more about this disability, in the 1960s it was barely recognized.) Though he retained nearly everything that he heard and was able to write, he could not read. To camouflage his condition, he used his sharp memory, keen listening skills, and quick wits and received As in the few subjects that did not bore him.

Bob received his first guitar at 14, a cheaply made acoustic model with strings so high off the neck it was almost impossible to play. He liked all kinds of music: the sugary vocals of the Kingston Trio, whose song "Tom Dooley" hit number one in the fall of 1958; the pop-swing harmonizing of the Everly Brothers on tunes like "Bye Bye Love"; the mischievous music of "Johnny B. Goode" himself, Chuck Berry. By the 1960s, Weir had also developed a liking for the plaintive vocals and guitar of folk star Joan Baez (a friend of Sarah Garcia).

As with Garcia, Weir's love for guitar playing spelled the end of his formal education. "I spent my last year in school learning to play guitar," he would say in a 1993 interview with David Gans of *Citadel Underground*. "Didn't attend a single class."

Weir's playing sounded rough to the banjo-playing

Grateful Dead guitarist Bob Weir. He met Garcia while both were guitar tutors at Dana Morgan's Music Store in Palo Alto. After an all-night jam session, they decided to form a band.

Garcia, but the skills Bob had learned to overcome dyslexia also helped him to develop an excellent ear for music. The two decided to form a really hip jug band, with guitar and banjo, harmonica, washboard, and kazoo.

Garcia and Weir first searched for a harmonica player. They found Ron McKernan, the son of a local radio deejay who had raised his kid on the same blues that he played for his listeners. The younger McKernan, whom everybody called "Pigpen," had grown up in northern California. Like Garcia and Weir, he had decided early on that music was far more interesting than school.

Though lacking formal training, McKernan had an intuition about music that no schooling could impart. And he had a stunning blues voice, as rough and strong as old oak.

Pigpen was everything his nickname suggested: coarse, stubbly, unkempt, and a little round in the face. He was a young man of boundless appetites, with a crazy streak that sometimes made him dangerous company: those who knew Pigpen gave him the wheel of a car at their own risk. The mustachioed McKernan dressed in jeans, shades, a cowboy hat, and a denim or leather jacket so frequently that the ensemble was practically a uniform.

Garcia next enlisted his friend David Nelson as a second guitarist and recruited two other area regulars to play washboard and kazoo. In 1964, the quintet—named Mother McCree's Uptown Jug Champions—began rehearsing in the basement of a Palo Alto house that Nelson rented for $15 a month.

Within a year, Mother McCree's antic mix of folk, bluegrass, jug tunes, and traditional blues had earned them a substantial local following. But McKernan urged his band mates to trade in the hillbilly-beatnik routine and go electric. Pigpen wanted to play the sort of loud, snarling blues that only a fully amplified band could perform. Eventually he persuaded the rest of the band to swing his way.

Other forces besides McKernan were influencing Mother McCree's. Rock and roll had foundered: Buddy Holly, Ritchie Valens, and the Big Bopper had been killed in a 1959 plane crash, and it seemed as though part of the music had died with them. The stars of the late 1950s already were beginning to fade, though some labored at "comebacks" or changed their sound to keep current. The energy and creativity of the moment seemed to belong instead to the rhythm and blues ("R & B") stars of the Motown label, like the Temptations and the Supremes, or to folk artists like Woodie Guthrie, Joan Baez, Bob Dylan, and Simon and Garfunkel.

The folk purists who found rock and roll so appallingly belligerent did not seem to mind the drought. They had long since closed their ears against these noisy, swaggering stylists anyway, all the while predicting the music's demise.

But rock and roll was not dying; it was just traveling abroad. The sound that had electrified America now stirred scores of British youths to take up guitars and drums and pound out the chords and backbeats to imported hits, such as Buddy Holly's "That'll Be the Day," Chuck Berry's "Maybelline," and Elvis Presley's "Heartbreak Hotel."

Naturally, the overseas rock and roll frenzy gave rise to British bands who had their own ideas about the sound. Word of a growing British rock scene brought American record executives overseas to watch young bands pack London or Liverpool clubs with screaming teens. Soon, American labels began signing British bands; first singles and then whole albums of British music began appearing in U.S. stores.

In 1964, rock and roll came roaring back home. The "British Invasion," a torrent of bands from the United Kingdom that hit the American music world in breathtaking succession—the Who, the Beatles, the Yardbirds, the Kinks, the Rolling Stones—would transform rock and roll for good.

No British rock band was more wildly celebrated than the Beatles, who became so huge that they even starred in their own film, *A Hard Day's Night*. Like thousands of young Americans, Jerry Garcia and Bob Weir

The Beatles perform on the *Ed Sullivan Show* in February 1964. The Beatles were the vanguard of the "British Invasion," a flood of British rock music inspired by Americans like Buddy Holly, Chuck Berry, and Elvis Presley.

saw the movie one night in 1964 and were dazzled. "What we saw them doing was impossibly attractive," Weir said. "I couldn't think of anything else more worth doing." The two even let their hair grow out in imitation of the mop-topped Liverpool boys.

It was the end of Mother McCree's Uptown Jug Champions. Pigpen had been half right, anyway. He wanted a switch—to blues. Garcia wanted to play rock and roll.

In search of a rhythm section, the new band discovered a gifted young drummer named Bill Kreutzmann, another teacher at Dana Morgan's. Bill had been a precocious player whose mother—a Stanford dance teacher—encouraged him. She would give her son an Indian tom-tom and let him tap out beats while she practiced her steps.

Soon after, the youngster was banging on his own set of drums. He grew so attached to the instrument that his father later had the drums sent to the Arizona prep school where his son was moping without them. By his early teens, Bill was teaching people older than he was and performing with bands. He was married and working as a stock clerk at Stanford Research Institute when Garcia and friends discovered him.

Finally, the group signed on Dana Morgan Jr., the store owner's son, as bass player. The elder Morgan agreed to outfit the band with the necessary equipment—guitars, drums, amplifiers, microphones, monitors, a mixing board, a public address (PA) system—and rehearsal space.

Calling themselves the Warlocks, Garcia, Weir, McKernan, Kreutzmann, and Morgan played their first gig in the spring of 1965 at Magoo's, a Menlo Park, California, restaurant. As Garcia remembered, they were an immediate success:

> [W]e had a huge crowd of people from the [local] high school, and they went . . . nuts! The next time we played, it was packed to the rafters. It was a pizza place. We said: "Hey, can we play in here [every] Wednesday night? We won't bother anyone. Just let us set up in the corner." It was *pandemonium*, immediately.

One member of the first night's audience was a musician named Phil Lesh, an acquaintance of Garcia who shared his enthusiasm for the Beatles and the Rolling Stones. Lesh was a musician as much by lineage as by choice. He remembered one day as a child being beckoned by his grandmother to his parents' living room to hear Brahms's First Symphony on the radio. To

Philip—just four years old—it sounded like a thunderstorm set to music. "The introduction comes on like the wrath of God," Lesh later explained. "It knocked me against the wall, figuratively speaking. I've never been the same since. As soon as I heard that, I knew—I just knew."

For the next four years, Philip was mesmerized by classical music. His father gave the third-grader a violin, and both parents endured the sour notes and errant squeals that were part of the boy's practice sessions. An unpopular kid, Phil spent a lot of time trying not to get beaten up by bigger, stronger kids. But he could play music better than any of his peers.

Philip played second violin in his school's orchestra when, at 14, he discovered that he preferred the trumpet. He flourished as a trumpeter: within a year, the gangly, fair-haired boy was performing lead parts in concertos and vying for the first chair at El Cerrito High School on the peninsula. Two years after that, he played trumpet in the second chair of Oakland Symphony—behind his own teacher. Rock and roll may have been storming the country, but Lesh was too absorbed in his studies to notice.

In college, Phil impressed teachers and classmates with his performing and arranging skills, and by the time he was 20 and a student at University of California at Berkeley, he had earned a reputation as an accomplished composer. His talent earned acclaim from peers but little money, however, so he worked through a string of day jobs in California and Nevada: as a librarian, a brokerage office assistant, a Las Vegas casino keno marker, a U.S. postal employee, and a radio engineer.

Lesh also dabbled in electronic music—a new sound that employed electrically amplified keyboards rewired to generate unique effects. While working for radio station KPFA, Lesh arranged to have the peninsula's premier banjo-playing beatnik—Jerry Garcia—per-

form live on a program called "The Midnight Special."

During his employment at the post office, Lesh had also seen *A Hard Day's Night* and had decided that if the Beatles could sport shaggy haircuts and be chased by screaming girls, well then, he could too. The new look did not impress his postal superiors, who dressed him down after receiving a customer complaint calling Lesh an "unkempt monkey."

Lesh didn't care. He was finally discovering rock and roll. Just before the Warlocks appeared at Magoo's,

Folk singers Joan Baez and Donovan waiting to perform during a 1965 "Peace in Vietnam" rally in London's Trafalgar Square. The musical style of the Grateful Dead grew out of traditional American folk, bluegrass, and country music, mixed with the new sound of rock and roll.

he told Garcia he might like to take up a rock and roll instrument. Garcia suggested the bass guitar. "I said, 'By God, I'll give it a try.'" Though Lesh had never played a bass in his life, he was hired, nudging out Dana Morgan Jr., who became the first and only ex-Warlock.

Garcia and Lesh made a strange pair: the dark-eyed, streetwise drifter and the giraffe-legged blond guy looking every bit the classical musician that he was. But Garcia knew that Lesh's skills in sound engineering, composing, arranging, and sight-reading would be a great asset to the band.

Without Morgan in the fold, the Warlocks had to return his father's equipment and find a new space in which to rehearse. They moved to another music store called Guitars Unlimited and, with some difficulty at first, began to arrange bookings as a blues-rock cover band doing standards like "Wooly Bully."

Before long, however, the band had moved away from jukebox hits and into a realm of its own. At venues like Frenchy's in Hayward and the In Room in Belmont, Warlock sets developed into long, loud blues jams with electric guitars cranked up as high as they could go.

At first the band's sound drove away more listeners than it attracted. Gradually, though, curious patrons who'd heard about this unique brand of heavy, spacey, blues-rock filtered into clubs where the Warlocks performed.

Their sound especially appealed to college students, artists, and bohemians weary of the same old pop. They wanted to break all the rules, and this included experimenting with illegal drugs and with a powerful (but still legal) chemical called lysergic acid diethylamide—LSD for short. And nearly everyone read Aldous Huxley's *The Doors of Perception*, viewed as a kind of primer on how to attain this chemically induced sixth sense.

The Warlocks themselves were no strangers to drug

use. Garcia had begun smoking marijuana in his teens. Lesh dropped LSD the night he saw the Warlocks at Magoo's. In part because of the tone of their music, Warlocks performances became perfect occasions to get stoned and to bathe in the sound; the band's wandering, ambient blues jams provided the perfect complement to an altered state of mind. Word got out that a Warlocks gig was more than just a rock and roll concert: it was an experience all its own.

3 ★ Playing in the Band

THE BEATNIKS OF THE 1950s believed that they lived in a dangerous and fragile world, where any hope of peace was undermined by
mutual hostility between the globe's predominant political and military
powers—the United States and the Soviet Union. For beatniks, the Cold
War was a waste of human spirit; it divided the world into "us" and "them."
But it was a cold, hard fact: family bomb shelters and a fearful, govern-
ment-run anticommunist crusade became as much a part of everyday
American life as Chevy convertibles and TV's *The Donna Reed Show*.

During the Cold War, the U.S. military committed billions of dollars
to researching plans of defense against enemy nations, including an uncon-
ventional—and top secret—exploration of the human mind and how it
could be manipulated. The military referred to such a possibility as "psy-
chological combat."

In one project, military scientists conducted a series of experiments
with "psychoactive" drugs, which alter the mood and behavior of the user.
(Alcohol, caffeine, and nicotine are relatively mild—and legal—psychoactive substances.) The project focused on lysergic acid diethylamide, which

The Grateful Dead in 1966 outside the "Chateau" in Haight-Ashbury. Clockwise from left: Bill
Kreutzmann, Bob Weir, Jerry Garcia, Pigpen McKernan, and Phil Lesh.

was first produced accidentally in 1938 by Dr. Albert Hoffman, a Swiss chemist seeking a new treatment for headaches. The military administered LSD in varying doses to paid volunteers under laboratory conditions to discover whether the drug could be an effective mind-control tool.

One of the volunteers was a struggling writer named Ken Kesey. An Oregon native, Kesey was a graduate student in creative writing at Stanford University who lived in a $60-a-month bungalow on Perry Lane, in the midst of the college bohemian crowd. For his participation in the LSD experiment, Kesey earned $75 a day at Menlo Park's Veterans Memorial Hospital.

Kesey was pleasantly startled by LSD's effects. He found the experience so mind-expanding, in fact, that he secured a job in the hospital's psychiatric wing, where he would have easy access to LSD and other psychedelic drugs. Enthusiastic over their effects, he began hosting parties in which he offered them as the main attraction. He may even have written his breakthrough novel, *One Flew Over the Cuckoo's Nest*, under the influence of LSD.

Meanwhile, the U.S. military had reluctantly concluded that LSD was not useful for Cold War defense. The drug was too "messy," inducing hallucinations and causing unpredictable reactions in test subjects. Some fell into waking trances. Others became highly animated and tried to act out their hallucinations. Many who were given high doses of LSD simply went berserk, screaming and convulsing in terror, sometimes for hours, as though trapped in nightmares. Far from making the human mind more controllable, the drug only made human behavior less predictable.

The official tests were thus discontinued. Kesey and his friends, however, had begun to view LSD, or "acid," as a tool for testing not only the outer boundaries of society but also the inner limits of the human mind.

They likened LSD's effects to that of peyote, a hallu-
cinogen derived from American cacti and used by some
Native Americans in religious ceremonies.

Military and government authorities were aware
that LSD had been manufactured outside their labora-
tories, but they took no action because its use did not
appear widespread. Thus, taking LSD during the 1950s
and early 1960s was not even a misdemeanor under the
law.

Augustus Stanley "Bear" Owsley III was one of
many "home chemists" manufacturing the psychedelic
drug after its use caught on. A sound engineer and elec-
tronics technician, Owsley established his own laboratory in Berkeley and distributed vitamin capsules of LSD
to his friends. One of the neighborhoods where LSD
was most popular was a favorite haunt of San Francisco's
young, hip crowd: the Haight-Ashbury district, named
for the intersection of its two major streets.

The Haight, as locals called it, was a warren of
crumbling Victorian houses adjacent to the rolling
lawns and exotic topiary of San Francisco's Golden Gate
Park. Once a wealthy district, the Haight had fallen into
disrepair when residents, alarmed by the growth of
nearby poor neighborhoods, began moving to the hills
overlooking San Francisco Bay.

But the area's charming and cheap housing
appealed to college kids, artists, poets, professors, and
young bohemians, all drawn by the possibility of making the neighborhood their own. Real-estate owners
took advantage of the renewed interest and carved up
many of these artful old wrecks into apartments.

Gathering on each other's doorsteps in cast-off
Edwardian waistcoats and strolling through Golden
Gate Park in shirts and pants of riotous colors, the new
residents brought energy and creativity to Haight-
Ashbury. The practice of tie-dyeing—creating flowery,
multi-hued designs by tying portions of fabric so they

do not absorb the dye—became a cottage industry in the Haight. The neighborhood came alive with new businesses: secondhand and handmade clothing stores; "head shops" that stocked paraphernalia for smoking marijuana and hashish; poster and printing businesses; bookstores specializing in obscure and arcane titles; theater and film venues with outlandish names like the Magic Theater for Madmen Only; and eateries like the Coexistence Bagel Shop, with poetry and music on the menu.

Often, businesses would combine services: the Blue Unicorn, for example, was run by a Naval Academy dropout who advertised "food, books, music, and art" and "no jukebox," and allowed patrons without money to wash dishes in exchange for food. Clad in denim jeans and paisley shirts, patrons would gather in spots like the Blue Unicorn to discuss music, art, literature, and current issues: the government's harsh treatment of Native Americans; the civil rights movement; or the U.S. war in Vietnam.

The peninsula was a hot spot of political dissidence during the 1960s, and a wide variety of publications, theater groups, artists' circles, and other businesses—including many in Haight-Ashbury—identified themselves with the antiwar, antiestablishment struggle. Many followed a simple maxim: "Question Authority."

Haight residents in particular adhered to these bohemian ideals, creating their own moral codes—though they were often financed by "establishment" parents, who imagined the money they sent was paying for school tuition and textbooks. By 1965, the *San Francisco Examiner*, drawing on the name given to untraditional jazz aficionados of the 1940s and 1950s—"hipsters"—referred to the young denizens of this subculture as "hippies."

Rock groups formed and multiplied like living cells in San Francisco in 1965: the Charlatans, the

Quicksilver Messenger Service, the Mystery Trend, the Marbles, Big Brother and the Holding Company, Country Joe and the Fish, the Final Solution, and Wildflower were among new bands launched that year. The city even boasted a nationally known act, the Jefferson Airplane, whose members included guitarist Jorma Kaukonen, an old jamming partner from Garcia's jug band days.

Concerts were scheduled almost every night, during which local groups would often perform with national acts in venues like the Fillmore Auditorium and the Avalon Ballroom. So much was happening that one local dance promoter, Luria Castell, predicted that San Francisco would become "the American

Ken Kesey's psychedelically patterned 1939 school bus. In 1964, he and the Merry Pranksters traveled from California to New York in the bus, which was outfitted with bunks and benches for living quarters. A ladder led to a hole in the roof, where a platform with a railing allowed riders to "hang out." The bus was wired for sound so that Pranksters could not only broadcast music outside, but also hear street sounds inside.

A group of mellow Merry Pranksters at an Acid Test. In the early 1960s, Jerry Garcia and Phil Lesh lived near Ken Kesey in the Haight and attended a number of his parties. The Warlocks first performed at an Acid Test in 1964, shortly before renaming themselves the Grateful Dead.

Liverpool," referring to the British town made famous by the Beatles.

Castell and her friends—fellow promoters Chet Helms, Jack and Ellen Harmon, and Alton Kelley—saw great promise in the burgeoning music scene of San Francisco and wanted to showcase the creative oddness of Haight-Ashbury. They formed a concert organizers group called the Family Dog, borrowing money from their parents to rent a longshoremen's union hall near Fisherman's Wharf in San Francisco. They hired musical performers, a disc jockey, and a visual artist to create a colorful light and slide show that projected swirly art in motion onto the walls, floor, and ceiling of the hall.

The Warlocks, now well into the Haight-Ashbury environment, attended the second Family Dog show out of curiosity. They discovered a kind of midnight circus, a strange carnival of music and visual effects coming from all directions. The Lovin' Spoonful, a New York band, was performing that night, while oddly dressed patrons—many high on marijuana or "tripping" on LSD—danced aimlessly, lost in the sound and the whirling colored lights. The whole event resembled Ken Kesey's Perry Lane parties on a grander scale. Lesh found Family Dog promoter Ellen Harmon and exclaimed, "Lady, what this little séance needs is us!"

Kesey, meanwhile, was now hosting parties all over northern California. He loved to bring together vastly diverse groups of people: artists and writers, college kids, and members of the Hell's Angels, the outlaw motorcycle gang. He embellished meeting places with bizarre artwork and a sound system that picked up both music and conversation and bounced them electronically across rooms. And of course, LSD was always in supply.

Kesey called such gatherings "Acid Tests" and his regular guests the "Merry Pranksters." He papered the peninsula with posters and leaflets asking, "Can You Pass the Acid Test?" and provided the willing with directions to the next party.

The Pranksters lived communally in a house in La Honda, California. The gang included Ken Babbs, a writer and former Marine helicopter pilot, and Neal Cassady, a wiry drifter with dark hair and blazing eyes who was the inspiration for Dean Moriarty in Jack Kerouac's *On the Road.*

In 1964, Kesey used his advance money from *One Flew Over the Cuckoo's Nest* to buy a school bus, which he decorated in neon colors and psychedelic patterns. He then took his friends on a spontaneous cross-country trek to the World's Fair in New York City, a Merry Pranksters mystery tour on two levels—one on the bus and one on LSD. With company like the maniacal driver Babbs behind the wheel and Cassady, the quintessential American wanderer, the bus became a rolling metaphor. "You're either on the bus or off," the Pranksters liked to say. There was no middle ground.

Though LSD was still legal at the time, using it "*felt illegal*," as writer Charles Perry noted, and it became more popular than military scientists would have imagined. In the East, former Harvard University professor Timothy Leary and a colleague were fired from their posts in 1963 for giving the drug to students. Undaunted, Leary promoted LSD use, founding his own magazine, the *Psychedelic Review*, and touring college campuses with his pro-LSD message, "Turn on, tune in, drop out."

But the lauded psychedelic drug also had a horrifying dark side. As LSD became more popular, young users began turning up in hospital emergency rooms after bad trips, whose side effects included convulsions, panic, and severe depression. Sometimes the pain would linger for hours—and would inexplicably return in head-twisting "flashbacks" days, weeks, months, or even years later. LSD can also induce psychotic reactions in users, which might compel them to violence, destruction, or even suicide.

During this time, Jerry Garcia and Phil Lesh lived a few blocks from Kesey's Perry Lane apartment in a group house known as the Chateau. They'd attended a few of Kesey's parties and sampled LSD there. Word of the Warlocks' reputation eventually reached Kesey through mutual Prankster friends, and they were invited to play at an Acid Test.

In 1964, the Warlocks released their first single on the locally based Scorpio label—covers of the old bluegrass standards "Stealin'" and "Don't Ease Me In." But they learned of an East Coast band also called the Warlocks and to avoid legal complications recorded a demo tape in November under the name "Emergency Crew" instead. (The band would re-release these songs under their new name in June 1966.)

Timothy Leary, with yellow flowers tucked behind his ears, at a Be-In in San Francisco.

Though Emergency Crew was acceptable temporarily, the band wanted a more unique name. They started tossing ideas around. Mythical Ethical Icicle Tricicle? Nonreality Sandwich?

Weeks of brainstorming passed. Then one day, Garcia opened an old dictionary, and a phrase caught his eye: "In the land of the dark," it read, "the ship of the sun is pulled by the Grateful Dead." The words came from an ancient Egyptian prayer, *The Book of the Dead.* Suddenly, all the other words on the page disappeared.

At first the band members thought it seemed too morbid, but soon the name began to sound better. After testing it on friends, they decided to try it out and see whether it caught on.

It did. The Grateful Dead—Garcia, Lesh, Weir, Kreutzmann, and McKernan—debuted on December 4, 1965, at Kesey's second Acid Test. With 400 people

A native of Berlin, events promoter Bill Graham staged one of the earliest multimedia events in rock history: the Trips Festival of 1966.

crammed into a house pulsing with guitar noise and colored lights, the rechristened band settled into a slow blues groove.

The Grateful Dead were not only "on the bus," as the Pranksters would say; they were the dashboard radio. They played a series of Acid Tests in Palo Alto and later at a house in Muir Beach, where Kesey's friend, LSD dealer Bear Owsley, heard their music for the first time.

"It scared me," Owsley would say years later. "They seemed to have . . . a connection to a very scary, very dangerous aspect of reality to me." But Bear also felt curiously drawn to the music of the Grateful Dead; the connection was so strong, in fact, that he moved in with them and became their benefactor.

San Francisco's night life during that time owed much of its vibrancy to a Berlin, Germany, native named Bill Graham. Graham and his family had fled Nazi Germany to the United States, where he was a corporate executive before deciding on a career as an events promoter for the avant-garde arts. A shrewd, manic fellow with a throaty voice and a brusque temperament, Graham loved theater. He was described by one hippie as "a cross between Mother Teresa and Al Capone," but he was well respected for his talent and his support of local artists and musicians.

In 1965, Graham was approached by his friend Stewart Brand, a photographer and sometime Prankster who had produced a multimedia show about Native Americans. Like Luria Castell, Brand wanted to stage a celebration of music, visual art, and lights, which he would call the Trips Festival. He asked for Graham's help.

And so it happened. On Friday, January 21, 1966, the Trips Festival opened at Longshoreman's Hall. Light shows, dancers, book stands, stage presentations, metal statues called Thunder Machines that sang when you touched them, stray microphones for public use, Acid Test subjects, live music—each "event" had its own room. The hall was packed with guests, and more waited outside in a line that snaked around the building.

Ken Kesey had been arrested the previous week for possession of marijuana and had been forbidden by court order to attend. Yet there he was, clad in an astronaut suit, admitting members of the motorcycle gang the Hell's Angels free of charge through a rear door. The Merry Pranksters arrived in colored leotards and capes trimmed with baubles—a tribute to their favorite comic-book heroes.

The Trips Festival ran for two days; the Grateful Dead was scheduled to play on Saturday, the second night. Garcia was given his cue: "Jerry Garcia! Plug in!" read the projector screen display above his head. But when Jerry got to the stage, he discovered that his guitar had been knocked over. Graham, clipboard in hand, saw Garcia onstage cradling the broken instrument and ran up to him.

To Garcia's amazement, Graham dropped to his knees and tried to fix the shattered instrument. But the guitar couldn't be repaired. The Dead did not play.

Despite such glitches, the Trips Festival was hailed by Haight residents and other attendees as a tremendous success, a happening without bounds. But word of this sensory carnival had also reached San Francisco politicians and police, who saw the burgeoning hippie phenomenon as a threat to the city's reputation and its well-being. In addition, many denizens of the Haight were children of prominent San Francisco citizens, who had alarmed their parents by dropping out of school and disappearing into the hippie subculture. In the eyes of many of these adults, this trend amounted to kidnapping—and they wanted it stopped.

Rock and roll was now a phenomenon that had worked its way into musical corners where no one expected to find it. In 1965, folk music star Bob Dylan shocked fans by replacing his acoustic guitar with an electric one to release the rock album *Bringing It All Back Home*. With songs like the tangled "Subterranean Homesick Blues" and the jangly "Mr. Tambourine Man," Dylan created a new genre known as folk rock and triggered a musical wave that performers like the Grateful Dead would ride to success.

By the summer of 1966, an estimated 15,000 self-styled hippies—many of them runaways—lived in the Haight-Ashbury district. Spurred by news of the strange and wonderful San Francisco scene, more arrived every week from around the country.

And the Grateful Dead were now busier than ever. They continued playing the Acid Test "circuit," from Portland, Oregon to Los Angeles. Garcia's own fondness for LSD became so well known that his friends nicknamed him "Captain Trips."

Not every Grateful Dead gig was an acid showcase, however. The Dead performed at a number of Trips-like benefit shows for local avant-garde and politically minded theater groups. They also played dances at the Fillmore and the old Avalon Ballroom, the latter run by promoter Chet Helms. Garcia, in fact, often referred to the group as a "dance band" that just happened to play 20-minute songs. Soon they were popular enough to attract the attention of the music industry.

One of the Dead's first suitors was a Warner Bros. executive named Joe Smith. "I came up and saw the Grateful Dead one night at an unforgettable evening at the Avalon," Smith recalled. "I'd never seen anything like that, never seen a light show or people freaking out like that. . . . I knew that our record company . . . could not afford to let the Grateful Dead go."

Wary of big, prestigious record companies like Warner Bros. and of everything they represented, the Dead hesitated to accept a contract. Fearful of "selling out," they insisted on total control of the final product. They even asked Smith to drop acid to listen to their music. (He gently declined.) Finally, after much haggling, the Grateful Dead signed on.

4 Are You Going to San Francisco?

IN SEPTEMBER 1966, the Grateful Dead—except Lesh and Kreutzmann—moved back to the house they had once occupied at 710 Ashbury Street. The peeling, four-story Victorian already housed band manager Rock Scully, who ran the Dead's business affairs there.

Haight-Ashbury continued to be the center of hippie culture. Politically radical crews like the Diggers and the Mime Troupe performed street theater and gave away food to newly arrived and penniless would-be hippies. An acid-head supply merchant called the Psychedelic Shop also published the leading hippie newspaper, the *Oracle*, which the Diggers frequently used as a platform for their blunt criticism of modern society.

The Haight had also become "center stage" for a musical pageant of crazy performances and new bands. In the wake of the Trips Festival, Bill Graham emerged as a key rock music promoter on the West Coast; he kept the Fillmore and the Winterland busy almost every night. And the Grateful Dead were fast becoming the house band of the Haight-Ashbury music world.

In the 1960s, rock dances were not advertised in newspapers. The only way to announce such events was by posting signs in and around the area where the concert would be held. In the musical explosion occurring in

The Grateful Dead pose in their Victorian-era home at 710 Ashbury Street in the Haight.

San Francisco, the business of creating eye-catching poster art grew rapidly. Haight-based illustrators and artists developed a psychedelic, pop-art style that was instantly collectible: their wildly colorful concert posters often disappeared almost as quickly as they went up.

The Grateful Dead were among the bands whose popularity had been enhanced by concert posters advertising their gigs. And as one of the premier rock bands of San Francisco, the Dead needed a visual image that fans would instantly associate with their music. For this project, they recruited Stanley Mouse, a California artist known for his airbrushed custom-car detailing and "hot rod art" T-shirt designs, and his partner, Family Dog member Alton Kelley.

Mouse had moved to the Bay area from Detroit, Michigan, in 1965, lured by the surf and the atmosphere of the Haight. He had brought with him his entire studio and a few members of "The Laughing Academy," an artists' hangout near the Art School of the Society of Arts and Crafts in Detroit. Mouse set up a T-shirt shop near Berkeley and hung out in San Francisco as often as he could, where he visited fellow ex-Detroiters like James Gurley, the guitarist of the new band called Big Brother and the Holding Company.

Mouse met Family Dog member and fellow hot-rod artist Alton Kelley during one of his visits to the city that year. Kelley had heard of Mouse's work and loved his signature cartoon character, "Freddy Flypogger." As it happened, Family Dog owner Chet Helms was in search of a poster artist for the Avalon's regular events, and Kelley persuaded him to take on Mouse. Before long, the two were working together: Kelley would do the research, supplying the ideas for overall images and design, while Mouse would execute the poster, fine-tuning the ideas until they formed a finished piece.

Mouse-Kelley Studios had already designed one poster for an August 1966 Grateful Dead concert at the

Avalon Ballroom when they were recruited to design a second one advertising a September concert at the Avalon. A swirling, art nouveau-style creation in yellow and black, the first poster centers around a "portrait" of Frankenstein's monster, whom the artists considered "one of the Grateful Dead." This juxtaposition of traditional graphics and offbeat visual humor became the trademark of the Mouse-Kelley house.

For their second Grateful Dead poster, the two set to work on a defining logo for the band. Inspired by the "live in the here and now" theme of 11th-century Persian poet Omar Khayyám's the *Rubáiyát* and by Edmund Sullivan's illustrations for it, Mouse developed the image of a human skeleton wearing a garland of red roses and carrying a wreath of the same.

The poster image has since become perhaps the most recognized visual representation of any rock group. The "skull and roses" design—and Mouse's countless variations upon it—was a visual translation of the elusive mysticism of the Grateful Dead's music.

On October 6, 1966, less than a month after the Dead concert advertised by the new poster, the state of California declared LSD illegal. (Similar rulings in other states eventually followed.) That same day, a crowd gathered in the San Francisco panhandle for an event billed as a "Love Pageant Rally," the purpose of which, according to the *Oracle*, was "to affirm [the] identity, community and innocence" of young hippies across the country. The Dead, Big Brother and the Holding Company, and Wildflower performed as the now-illicit LSD was passed around—albeit more discreetly than before.

Undercover narcotics officers swarmed the grounds looking for Kesey, who was now a felon, but though the Pranksters' crazy-colored bus idled in plain sight, Kesey was not there. Meanwhile, the Grateful Dead performed a tongue-in-cheek tribute to their benefactor (and LSD manufacturer) Owsley in a song called "Alice D.

Millionaire."

Not long after, Kesey was arrested for drug possession. Before he was sentenced, he conducted a
Halloween-night "Acid Test Graduation," complete
with mock diplomas. A subdued Kesey told the attendees that it was time to move on. "This doesn't mean
stop taking acid," he said in his "commencement
address." But it was time to do something with the
experience.

The Grateful Dead were on part of a double bill
that night at California Hall with Quicksilver
Messenger Service and did not attend the graduation.
But among the members of Anonymous Artists, whom
Kesey booked instead, was Sarah Ruppenthal, whose
marriage to Jerry Garcia was ending. (Ruppenthal
would obtain custody of their daughter Heather.)
Garcia had grown close to Carolyn Adams, a young
woman from a well-to-do New York family who came
west as a teenager and fell in with the Pranksters. Neal
Cassady nicknamed her "Mountain Girl."

The success of the Love Pageant Rally inspired
plans for an even bigger hippie festival. The "Human
Be-In" or "Gathering of the Tribes" took place on
January 14, 1967. Colorful hand-lettered banners
bobbed above the 20,000 fans dressed in hippie finery
who filled Polo Field stadium in Golden Gate Park.
They trance-danced wildly to the music of hometown
bands like Big Brother and the Holding Company, the
Jefferson Airplane, the Sir Douglas Quintet, and the
Grateful Dead, while a Zen Buddhist priest meditated
silently onstage.

That winter, the Grateful Dead traveled to Los
Angeles to record their first album. Because they refused
to submit to the sort of meticulous studio grooming
they associated with straight music, the band finished
recording in three days. But the truth, as even band
members would later admit, was that their self-titled

debut would have benefited from some studio polish. Released in 1967, *Grateful Dead* did reflect the band's live sound, a seemingly aimless ramble through blues solos, cover tunes, and freaky compositions reflecting the Haight-Ashbury life. But the sound did not translate well to vinyl, and the album was a less-than-spectacular debut for a band with such a rapidly growing fan base.

Despite its flaws, however, the album allowed the Dead and other local bands to reach new listeners outside the San Francisco area. A local FM radio station, KMPX, began playing singles from the Dead's album, and with radio play and the publicity of events like the Be-In, the adventurous San Francisco sound spread far beyond northern California.

In Los Angeles, the capital of popular music, the new sound was impossible to ignore. While the Byrds and Crosby, Stills, & Nash personified the Los Angeles sound, the Jefferson Airplane, the Grateful Dead, and

A peddler of incense walks among fans at the San Francisco Love Pageant Rally on October 6, 1966—the same day that the state of California declared LSD illegal.

Rock singer Janis Joplin performs with her band, Big Brother and the Holding Company, during the Monterey Pop Festival in June 1967.

Big Brother and the Holding Company—now fronted by an electrifying blues singer from Texas named Janis Joplin—embodied the San Francisco hippie rock-blues sound.

But the two premier music scenes remained largely segregated. In fact, a musical rivalry had sprung up between Los Angeles and San Francisco, and differing styles were only part of the reason. Northern bands like the Grateful Dead considered live performances the true test of a rock group's mettle. They thought the "Los Angeles sound" was that of money changing hands, a slick, get-rich-quick philosophy that matched the music and did not fare well on stage.

Los Angeles bands were just as disdainful of San Francisco music. John Phillips, the lead singer of the Los Angeles quartet the Mamas and the Papas, was among them. But Phillips thought that the time was right to combine the sounds in a sort of rock and roll showcase—a huge weekend festival of the world's best bands, with proceeds donated to charity. The location: Monterey, California—halfway between San Francisco and Los Angeles.

The plan was bold, unprecedented—and seemingly impossible to carry out. The logistics of rallying bands from the two California cities—let alone Europe—were more than intimidating; they were nearly unfathomable. But as 1967 progressed, it became clear that Phillips was going to have his way. Or at least part of his way.

For the tricky business of convincing San Francisco groups to participate, Phillips enlisted an "outsider"—his friend Paul Simon, a New York singer-songwriter. Simon could hardly believe his senses when he arrived in the Haight. Hippies filled the streets and parks, parading in ragged clothes, smiling at him while openly smoking marijuana. He nervously declined several offers of a puff of this or a hit of that as Rock Scully escorted him through the neighborhood to 710 Ashbury, where the Grateful Dead waited.

Simon picked his way through a cluster of people on the stairwell outside, walked into the house, and asked the ringleaders of the San Francisco rock scene to consider playing in a Los Angeles-organized festival called "Monterey Pop."

The Dead did not respond graciously. In fact, Simon's presentation went badly. He was still reeling from the experience when he phoned Phillips in Los Angeles that night. In his 1986 autobiography, Phillips remembers Simon telling him,

> It's the spookiest place I've ever seen and these people are the strangest people I have ever encountered in my life. . . . Jerry Garcia, Bob Weir, Pigpen—man, it's strange up here. I'm sure they're all stoned. They sit around and riff all day. The girls do the chores and the guys work on the music. It's like they're suburban kids underneath it all.

But the Dead had agreed to do the show—with a list of conditions. "The Dead want Janis [Joplin] on the bill; they want Big Brother and the Airplane and

Quicksilver," Simon recounted; "they want their own night to do their thing—the final night."

The Monterey Pop Festival ran from June 16 to 18, 1967, with more than two dozen acts performing for a crowd of about 90,000. As they had demanded, the Grateful Dead shared the final night with a dazzling lineup, including R & B singer Otis Redding, Booker T. and the MGs, guitar wizard Jimi Hendrix, the Who, the Steve Miller Band, the New Animals, Electric Flag, Laura Nyro, Canned Heat, Quicksilver Messenger Service, Jefferson Airplane, Country Joe and the Fish, the Mamas and the Papas, the Byrds, Buffalo Springfield, and sitar player Ravi Shankar, among others.

The Dead's performance was not particularly memorable—equipment trouble plagued the band all night. And tickets to the festival had been so oversold that hundreds of people were stopped at the gate. But, true to the spirit of the hippie movement, Phil Lesh persuaded concert organizers to admit free of charge all those who had been turned away. In addition, the Dead later held a series of free, post-Monterey jam sessions with several other musicians at a nearby campus.

For all its shortcomings, Monterey Pop marked a milestone in rock music history. The San Francisco sound finally played to a major audience. At the same time, the festival itself promoted the concept of staging rock mega-concerts; the phenomenon would spread during the remainder of the 1960s and is no doubt the origin of the grand concert productions we are accustomed to attending today.

The music showcased at Monterey formed a kind of soundtrack for what became known as the "Summer of Love," an outpouring of inspired new rock released in 1967 that included the Beatles' psychedelia-tinged *Sergeant Pepper's Lonely Hearts Club Band*; *Blowin' Your Mind* by Van Morrison; *Are You Experienced?*, the smash debut of the Jimi Hendrix Experience; and the self-

titled first album of the Doors.

But in the Haight, the Summer of Love was becoming a season of discontent. The now-famous neighborhood teemed with newcomers, including thousands of runaway kids; its original glow was fading fast. In the first half of 1967 alone, some 50,000 people streamed into the hippie stronghold; by autumn, the Haight's population reached 75,000.

The flood of new arrivals overwhelmed the neighborhood. The Diggers tried to accommodate the homeless by setting up a soup kitchen, but no one in the Haight was equipped to keep up with the demand for food, housing, clothing—or dope. Homeless teenagers began sleeping in the Panhandle and Golden Gate Park. The crime rate rose; Haight merchants were furious over increased losses.

And everyone wanted to hang out with the Grateful Dead, who had truly become the neighborhood band. The door of 710 Ashbury was always open. "It was sort of a community center," said band manager Rock Scully, describing the swarms of visitors:

The Grateful Dead with managers Rock Scully and Dan Rifkin (center) during a press conference following the arrest of Weir, McKernan, and Scully for marijuana possession. The Dead criticized the California law that made drug possession a felony. The charges were ultimately dropped.

It got so busy that we had to take over 715 across the street. It was almost impossible to get any business done there [at 710]. . . . The house was jammed packed all the time. . . . the front steps were always crowded with people. The whole neighborhood was very social that way. Janis and Big Brother lived down the street. The Charlatans lived in the neighborhood. The Airplane and Quicksilver would always stop by. Our house became a center of activity, and there was always something going on.

In the eyes of the law, *too* much was going on. On October 2, 1967, officers raided the house and arrested Weir, McKernan, Scully, and several others for marijuana possession (a felony under California law) and confiscated the files of a free legal clinic working out of the same address. Angered by the bust, the Grateful Dead held a press conference blasting the police for harassing the clinic and for the drug raid itself: "These arrests were made under a law that classifies smoking marijuana with murder, rape, and armed robbery," the band's statement read. Though the charges ultimately were dropped, the message from the Establishment, unhappy with the hippie population explosion, was clear: We're watching.

The rest of the world was watching too: national news magazines like *Newsweek* and *Time* had begun to take note of the Haight-Ashbury culture. Jerry Garcia interviewed with CBS News. A local tour bus company promoted "Hippie Hops" through the Dead's home turf and drove by 710 Ashbury, although the tours were scrubbed when disgusted Haight residents began pelting the buses with rotten vegetables.

In the midst of the uproar of 1967, the Grateful Dead completed their second album, *Anthem of the Sun*, in New York. They enlisted the help of an old friend, Tom Constanten, for keyboards, songwriting, and arranging, and added a second percussionist, Mickey Hart. But the sessions were so fractious that producer

Dave Hassinger quit before the album was finished, and the band aggravated Warner Bros. with its overspending.

Shortly after Christmas, Warner Bros. vice president Joe Smith sent Dead comanager Danny Rifkin a sharply worded letter, blasting the band for its unprofessional behavior and branding the album the "most unreasonable project with which we have ever involved ourselves." The Grateful Dead, he said, had become "an undesirable group in almost every recording studio in Los Angeles. . . . their attitudes and their inability to take care of business . . . would lead us to believe that they never will be truly important."

The completed album was a mystical hippie tour de force as indulgent as their debut, though far more exotic sounding. Many songs on Anthem are presented as suites, as with classical chamber music, with subtitled passages such as "Cryptical Envelopment" or "Quadriplet for Tender Feet," in which guitar-based music is embroidered with the sounds of finger cymbals, crotales (rattles), and a celesta—a keyboard instrument with hammers that strike steel plates. Grateful Dead fans eagerly snatched up the record.

In addition to regular venues like the Avalon Ballroom, the Dead also held free concerts in the city's parks and on closed-off streets. Performing on makeshift stages made of flatbed trucks parked side by side, and often without proper permits, they drew hundreds of fans to each show. But such concerts became increasingly difficult to stage when city authorities began enforcing more strictly the laws restricting public gatherings without permits.

The band played its last outdoor show in the area on March 3, 1968, overlooking Haight Street and a sea of hippies. "[I]t was a big block party," Carolyn Adams recalled. "So the street was closed to traffic and, instead, packed with people. It was beautiful."

5 ★ Truckin'

HAIGHT-ASHBURY FINALLY BECAME TOO MUCH even for Jerry Garcia. In the winter of 1968, he and Carolyn moved to a house in Marin County, in a pocket of redwood forest called Larkspur. They were joined by an old Garcia confidant, Robert Hunter.

Garcia had met Hunter after his army discharge, and the two had shared a house near Perry Lane. Hunter had played bass in one of Garcia's early bluegrass outfits and wrote some of the lyrics for *Anthem of the Sun*— most notably the 15-minute song, "Alligator."

Like Kesey, Hunter had participated in the military's LSD tests at Menlo Park's Veterans Memorial Hospital. One of his early songs, "China Cat Sunflower," is an especially good example of the romantic, moody, and surreal writing style he developed in part from his experience:

> Krazy Kat peeking through a lace bandanna
> Like a one-eyed Cheshire, like a diamond eye jack
> A leaf of all colors plays a golden string fiddle
> To a double-e waterfall all over my back.

Joe Cocker performs during the "three days of peace, love, and music" at Woodstock in August 1969. With over 400,000 fans and two dozen acts, the acid- and rain-drenched festival made history. "You definitely knew that this was a milestone," Garcia remarked 25 years later. "But our performance . . . was musically a total disaster that is best left forgotten."

Garcia was so enchanted by Hunter's writing that he asked him to serve as the Dead's "lyricist in residence," in the tradition of British rock groups like Procol Harum.

Hunter's dreamy metaphors fit nicely into the Grateful Dead's wandering, exploratory sound. Garcia and Hunter became full-time collaborators in early 1968, when they cowrote several songs for the Grateful Dead's third album, *Aoxomoxoa*, a nonsensical palindrome (a word reading the same forward or backward) that Hunter devised.

The album was recorded over eight months and left the Dead $100,000 in debt to Warner Bros.—largely because the Dead insisted on employing expensive new technology. They recorded on a 16-track rather than the traditional 4-track system, laying down 16 separate layers of sound onto one master reel. The result was an auditory opulence that older technology could not match. Even the Beatles' lavishly orchestrated *Sergeant Pepper* album, for example, had been recorded on only 4 tracks.

But *Aoxomoxoa* did not contain a short pop-style tune that Warner Bros. could release as the first single. By now the label's executives were so frustrated with the band that they were ready to abandon the project altogether. Finally, they agreed to release the album on one condition: the Dead would next cut a live album culled from recorded concerts.

Aoxomoxoa was released in 1969 to disappointing sales. The perfectionist Garcia would later refer to some of the album's songs as "cumbersome," "overwritten," or "marginal," though two numbers, "Dark Star" and "St. Stephen," eventually became live standards for the band. After all, the Grateful Dead was still a touring band, a hippie caravan bringing the original spirit of Haight-Ashbury to other parts of the world.

But the hippie utopia itself was collapsing. Strongly

addictive drugs like heroin had become commonplace in the Haight, and many idealistic newcomers ended up exploited by drug dealers, hooked on narcotics, or forced into dealing or prostitution to make money to supply their habits. Garcia later reflected on the change in atmosphere:

> It [had been] a very high, healthy kind of thing—there were no hard drugs, only pot and LSD. No rip-offs— none of that kind of stuff. No shootings, no knifings, no bombings, no explosions. Then when the big media flash came out—when the *Time* magazine guys came out and interviewed everybody and took photographs, and made it news—the feedback from that killed the whole scene. It was ridiculous.

The Haight acknowledged its failure to cope by staging a weekend ceremony in October 1968, called the "Death of the Hippie." Residents held a mock wake at a local church and marched in a "funeral procession" down Buena Vista Hill bearing the effigy of a hippy. Grateful Dead drummer Bill Kreutzmann carried a large wooden cross.

The dire ceremony preceded a shakeup among Grateful Dead members. Garcia fired Weir and McKernan that fall and formed the quartet "Mickey Hart and the Heartbeats," named after the newest band member, drummer Mickey Hart. Bill Kreutzmann would also play drums, providing the basic rhythm line, with Lesh on bass and Garcia, of course, on guitar. The Dead, always striving to be different, were now a two-drummer band.

Mickey Hart had grown up surrounded by drums: both parents were percussionists, and his father, Lenny, also ran a busy drum clinic in San Carlos, California. Hart had met Kreutzmann at a performance by jazz artist Count Basie in Haight-Ashbury and soon after sat in on one of the Grateful Dead's gigs. "And after that he just seemed to fit in," Kreutzmann recalled. Like the Dead, the music of the Heartbeats was experimental, but much more jazz tinged: the "acid rock" of the Grateful Dead had evolved into the "acid lounge" music of the Heartbeats.

But the new band was short lived; after a brief tour, the Grateful Dead reprised—with Weir and McKernan—at a three-day festival in upstate New York, another "gathering of the tribes" known as the Woodstock Music and Arts Festival. Unlike Monterey, spectators at Woodstock would stay the weekend: accommodations were set up on the grounds of a dairy farm in Saugerties, New York, where the concert would be held, so that every fan could enjoy the full "three days of peace, love, and music."

Some 400,000 rock fans attended the festival, which ran not three but four days, from August 15 to 18, 1969, mostly under a downpour of biblical intensity. Over two dozen acts performed, including many of those who had played at Monterey: Jimi Hendrix, the Jefferson Airplane, the Who, the Byrds, and others.

The Grateful Dead could not have asked for a more perfect audience than the crowd at Woodstock. But as with the Monterey Pop Festival, they were bedeviled by problems—more equipment failures and electrical storms. The Dead slogged through an uninspired set. Garcia recalled the experience:

We were on a metal stage and it was raining to boot and I was high and I saw blue balls of electricity bouncing across the stage and leaping onto my guitar when I touched the strings. No kidding—and all of the intercom and CB radio, all that communication all came through the amplifiers, every bit of it. And there were helicopters buzzing by, drowning out everything. There was this hysterical rumor going round; guys

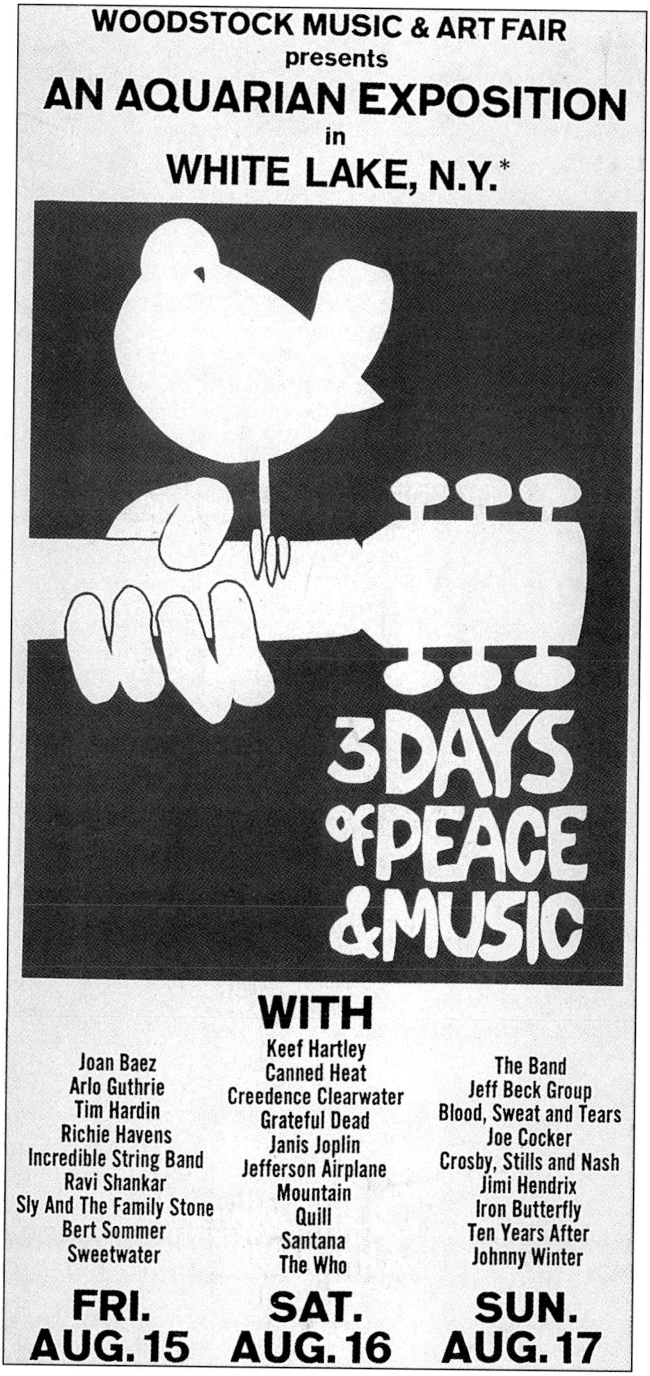

The original poster ad for the Woodstock festival.

Eager fans storm the gates at the ill-fated Altamont Speedway concert in December 1969. Several fans were attacked and one was killed by the Hell's Angels security force hired for the event.

yelling over the back of my amplifier, "The stage is collapsing! The stage is collapsing!"

The size of the crowd and the length of the festival turned Woodstock into a city in miniature, the capital of a psychedelic nation. In the course of the festival, 3 people died, 2 were born, and 33 were arrested on drug possession charges. It was a muddy, acid-drenched, elemental mess. But it made history: people came as concertgoers and left as members of the Woodstock generation.

"You definitely knew that this was a milestone, it was in the air," Garcia said in 1994, on the 25th anniversary of the Woodstock festival. "But our performance . . . was musically a total disaster that is best left forgotten. I've certainly been trying to forget it for 25 years."

Four months after Woodstock, another free-of-charge "pageant" of bands was slated for December 6 in San Francisco's Golden Gate Park, organized with the help of the Rolling Stones. Scheduling problems with the park forced Owsley and other organizers to move the event to a backup site outside the city limits—the Altamont Speedway, where local demolition derbies were held.

Owsley had a very bad feeling about Altamont. On a preconcert tour of the grounds, he thought, "This place smells of death. . . . This is the worst possible place to hold something like this."

Unfortunately, Owsley's premonition was confirmed. The messy, sodden Woodstock festival at least had been peaceful. Altamont, on the other hand, was a nightmare. Members of the Hell's Angels, hired as a security force, instead attacked and beat concertgoers without provocation. During the Rolling Stones's evening performance, one biker stabbed to death a young black man, Meredith Hunter, in front of the stage.

As for the Grateful Dead, they left Altamont without playing a note. Earlier in the day, a Dead crew member had been punched out by one of the Angels, leaving band members too shaken and angry to perform. "It was completely unexpected," Garcia said of the Altamont tragedy. "And that was the hard part—that was the hard lesson there—that you can have good people and good energy and work on a project and really want it to happen right and still have it all weird. It's the thing of knowing less than you should have. Youthful folly."

Writer Charles Perry summed up the Altamont concert as "the symbolic dead end of a generation's adventure." It was the end of a hard year as well. In 1969, Rolling Stones guitarist Brian Jones died of an overdose. In southern California, a former Haight resident named Charles Manson instructed his "followers"—runaways, loners, and disaffected teens much like those of Haight-Ashbury—to commit a series of ruthlessly brutal slayings, including the murder of actress Sharon Tate. Farther north, a makeshift "People's Park" in Berkeley was destroyed by local police and National Guardsmen carrying tear gas and shotguns. And on the other side of the world, a U.S. Army lieutenant was charged with a massacre of civilians in the Vietnamese village of My Lai, another flashpoint in the raging controversy over America's involvement in the war.

In February 1970, according to the agreement with Warner Bros., the Grateful Dead released *Live Dead*, a double album of live performance recordings that finally presented the Dead in their natural habitat—on stage. But the hippie spirit of the 1960s that had inspired these performances seemed to have evaporated. Even the house at 710 Ashbury was empty now. The band's business office had moved to the suburbs.

For the Grateful Dead, leaving the Haight was a transition, not an ending. Garcia had never considered himself an apostle of the hippie creed anyway; he only wanted to play good music and give listeners a good time. The Grateful Dead were never politically strident like the Diggers or vigilant like the editors of the *Oracle* and its cousin, the *Berkeley Barb*. "The thing about us, I guess, is that we're not really layin' anything on anybody," Garcia explained.

The misfortunes of 1969 seemed to continue into the new decade. In 1970 the legendary Beatles disbanded; Jimi Hendrix and Janis Joplin both died that fall of drug overdoses. The "old order" of rock and roll was fading. For the Grateful Dead, this was all the more reason to fight to survive. "Whenever there are times of stress," Garcia mused, "entertainment trips go way up. People need it; you gotta have something to get high with."

Ill fortune affected Dead members as well.

The cover design of the Grateful Dead's *Europe '72* three-album set, released in 1973 following their international tour, included the Mouse-Kelley Studios image of the "Ice Cream Kid" (left) and the "Rainbow Foot." The images were also combined to form a promotional poster for the album.

"Summer of 1970 was just one diabolical bummer after another," Garcia told an interviewer two years later. "Phil [Lesh]'s father died of cancer, my mother died in an automobile accident. . . . it was just like there was death happening. . . . So there we were in the studio, creating this thing, pullin' together."

The result was *Workingman's Dead*, an album of countrified blues and a striking departure from the group's usual acid rock. The spare, acoustic arrangements and contemplative lyrics, such as those in the multilayered "Uncle John's Band," reflect the band's struggle to find peace in a disorderly and damaged world:

Well, the first days are the hardest days
Don't you worry anymore
'Cause when life looks like easy street
There is danger at your door.

In "New Speedway Boogie," Garcia addresses the Altamont tragedy and its aftermath, declaring in a brittle voice, "One way or another, this darkness has got to give." And "Casey Jones," a slow, loping tune about the hazards of road life, became one of the band's most popular songs.

The Grateful Dead followed up later in the year with another collection of country-blues boogie, *American Beauty*, containing the now-classic singles "Sugar Magnolia," "Box of Rain," and "Truckin'"—a story of the Dead being busted by police earlier that year in New Orleans. "Lately it occurs to me," wrote Hunter in this last song, "what a long, strange trip it's been."

Workingman's Dead and *American Beauty* supplied the high that Garcia felt everyone needed to relieve stress. The band had refined their psychedelic Haight-Ashbury stew into a cleaner version of the stream-of-consciousness rock that they had pioneered.

They didn't stop there. Garcia, Lesh, Hart, and guitarist David Nelson also established a second, country-style band, the New Riders of the Purple Sage, which opened for the Dead during their concert tour—so members of both bands performed twice during each show.

In 1971, the Dead released a second collection of live recordings, a double-album set innocuously titled *The Grateful Dead* (not to be confused with their 1967 debut *Grateful Dead*)—the Dead's original title idea, an expletive, was nixed by Warner Bros. The album cover was the first to feature what would become the quintessential Grateful Dead emblem—Stanley Mouse's design of a human skull garlanded in red roses—and earned the album the nickname "Skull and Roses."

The album was a landmark in another way: the words "Dead Freaks Unite!" printed on the inside sleeve of the album cover marked the first concerted campaign to recognize the band's vast but familial following. There were quite a few "freaks" out there: the Grateful Dead sold a Dead record of 1.5 million copies, and the "Dead Freaks" rallying cry convinced 30,000 fans to sign on to the band's mailing list.

But more trouble was ahead. In 1971, Mickey Hart's father, Lenny, who had replaced Rock Scully as the Dead's manager, embezzled $70,000 from the group before being arrested and convicted. A humiliated Mickey Hart quit the band shortly afterward.

In September, longtime band member Pigpen McKernan was hospitalized for liver damage and forced to leave the band to recuperate. His departure stripped the Grateful Dead of his distinctive rusty growl and his agile harmonica, guitar, and keyboard work. Pigpen's salty blues style balanced the space-walking guitar solos of Jerry Garcia. He "had no discipline," Garcia later said, "but he had reams of talent," and much more:

> [H]e had that magical thing of being able to make stuff up as he went along. He also had great stage presence. The ironic thing was he hated [performing]. . . . His best performances were one-on-one, sitting in a room with an acoustic guitar. That's where he was really at home and at his best.

The Dead did not attempt to replace Pigpen; instead, they hired a keyboard player named Keith Godcheaux and his wife, vocalist Donna Godcheaux.

A jazz pianist, Keith was just beginning to explore blues and rock. He met Donna, a native southerner, through a mutual friend during a day hike into the mountains, and they were married soon after. Donna's father played guitar and sang on Texas radio stations; as a child she had accompanied her mother to an Alabama studio to watch recording sessions. Donna herself had performed with some of the most famous vocalists of the time: soul diva Aretha Franklin, R & B crooner Boz

Ron "Pigpen" McKernan, one of the original Grateful Dead. Years after Pigpen's death in 1973 of liver disease, Jerry Garcia described his continuing influence on band members: "He was a lovable person. Really, it hasn't felt quite right since Pigpen's been gone, but on the other hand . . . he hasn't been entirely gone. He's right around."

Scaggs, hit-makers Percy Sledge and Sam Cooke, and the "King of Rock and Roll" himself, Elvis Presley.

Keith and Donna were avid Dead fans. One night, while the band was on a break between sets at a Berkeley hangout called the Keystone, Donna Godcheaux approached Garcia backstage. The two somehow talked their way into attending a Grateful Dead rehearsal the following Sunday. Garcia, Kreutzmann and Keith Godcheaux wound up jamming for hours. "The two of us threw him every curveball we could," Kreutzmann remembers, "but he was right on every improvised change." On Monday, the whole band practiced with the couple, Donna recalls, "and by the end of that day, Keith was on the payroll."

Donna joined the Dead the following year, in a debut performance at a March 1972 Hell's Angels party in New York City. There they were: the southern girl and the Haight-Ashbury boys; the practiced vocalist and the guys who sang well enough to get by; the seasoned studio artist with little live experience and a band that practically lived on the road. But the Dead thrived on unlikely collaborations. The new formation seemed to work.

Later that year, Pigpen rejoined the band for its first overseas tour. But he was not well. "[W]e could sort of feel him slipping away a little. He was emaciated," Kreutzmann recalled. Pigpen died on March 6, 1973, of liver disease.

Years later, Garcia recalled Pigpen's powerful influence on his friends, band mates, and fans:

> It's hard for me to say what it was about him that people really loved.... I know I loved him a lot, and I couldn't begin to tell you why. He was a lovable person. Really, it hasn't felt quite right since Pigpen's been gone, but on the other hand he's always been around a little, too. He hasn't been entirely gone. He's right around.

In 1973 the Grateful Dead released a three-album collection of their tour performances, *Europe '72*. The band that had performed badly enough at Monterey and Woodstock to be excluded from documentary films of the events was now staging its own concerts and creating its own "documentaries" on vinyl. And the growing number of Dead Freaks proved that, despite the tragedies and difficulties of recent years, the Grateful Dead would go on.

6 ★ Estimated Prophet

THOUGH HIPPIES AND POST-WOODSTOCK GYPSIES still occupied Haight-Ashbury during the 1970s, pilgrimages from other parts of the country had ceased. Many burned-out residents, stung by memories of the Haight in its heyday, had begun moving to other parts of California. The corner of Haight and Ashbury Streets became a tourist stop where visitors posed for pictures under intersecting street signs.

The San Francisco sound that had developed during the Haight's hippie golden age was also changing. The death of Janis Joplin left her band, Big Brother and the Holding Company, without a future. Quicksilver Messenger Service disbanded. The Jefferson Airplane transformed itself into the Jefferson Starship, a band that critics would crucify as slick—with a small "s"—and uninspired. And former San Francisco regulars like the Charlatans, Wildflower, and the Final Solution were long gone. Of the purveyors of the Haight-Ashbury sound, the Grateful Dead was now the sole survivor.

Fans didn't seem to mind that the Dead were playing in a vacuum, though. The band toured relentlessly during the 1970s, and their following continued to grow. Using an Owsley-rigged sound system, the band per-

The back cover of *Grateful Dead from the Mars Hotel*, one of two 1974 albums. Shortly after *Mars Hotel* was released, the Grateful Dead stopped touring to focus on other business ventures. They resumed in June 1976.

formed nearly every day on stages decorated in psychedelic Americana and skull-and-roses motifs, with speak-
ers and amplifier covers decorated by San Francisco tie-
dye artist Courtenay Pollock.

Traditionally a live band, the Grateful Dead taped
nearly all of their shows—and so did many fans. To pro-
tect their music and control its distribution, most performers discourage amateur taping of their performances. But the Grateful Dead saw audience taping as a
trade-off: though they might sacrifice potential album
sales, they would continually attract fans to paying concerts where taping was permitted and had even become
part of the concert experience. Many fans still argue
that taping a Dead concert became so essential that
without it the Dead might have lost their following. To
the end, the live show remained the defining Dead
experience, the gathering place for Dead Freaks.

By the early 1970s, the Dead were playing nearly
every night to sold-out concerts across the United
States and Europe. Loyal fans began reappearing during
each tour, and many attended every night of a two- or
three-night stand. These ardent Grateful Dead fans
earned their own nickname: Deadheads.

Originally, Deadheads were young fans who identified with the sense of freedom and peaceful adventure
that defined the hippie experience. They flocked to
Dead shows in numbers that amazed Garcia and friends.
Every night on tour seemed to be another Be-In,
another Acid Test, the Haight transported, its tie-dyed
hippie colors intact and displayed by new fans.
Particularly avid Deadheads would even abandon their
home lives during Grateful Dead tours, piling into their
Volkswagen "bugs" and vans and following the band to
each concert on the tour.

The Grateful Dead became the "grand marshals" of
a long, strange parade that was mystifying—and frankly
irritating—to outsiders. Hadn't the '60s ended? Why

does this band still exist? And why were so many of their songs 20 minutes long? Deadheads and others of the Woodstock generation seemed to many a bunch of misguided flower children who had betrayed their country by opposing the Vietnam War.

Grateful Dead concerts grew so popular that local authorities in tour cities often would gird themselves for trouble when the hippie caravan arrived. To them, a Dead concert meant traffic jams, littering, drug busts and overdoses, strangers passed out on lawns—and another opportunity for local teenagers to disappear into the Deadhead fold.

Some towns reacted by turning up "the heat"—a hippie expression for police—when the Grateful Dead arrived. Camping permits suddenly became scarce, and concert crowds teemed with undercover narcotics officers. And nailing Deadheads for drug possession was no more difficult than catching fish in a hatchery: LSD hits, painted in psychedelic colors and condensed onto perforated paper sheets, were distributed like candy; marijuana smoke would cloud the air.

Even the grounds surrounding a concert venue were often heavily patrolled. Local police set up speed traps, alcohol spot checks, and other gauntlets for incoming fans. A Grateful Dead bumper sticker on one's vehicle was practically a printed invitation to be pulled over and searched by police. Careless but generally harmless Deadheads even ended up in local jail cells while their beloved band performed.

During all the hubbub, Jerry Garcia and Bob Weir released solo albums: *Garcia* and *Ace*, respectively, both in 1972. The Grateful Dead backed Weir on *Ace*—Dead fans heard Donna Godcheaux before they ever saw her perform—and Garcia teamed up with his resident lyricist, Hunter, on his Dead-like solo debut.

It was an eventful year. The band's Warner Bros. contract had just expired and Warner rival Columbia

Members of a Grateful Dead caravan during a summer festival in New York. Deadheads began following the band from town to town to attend every performance. Concert crowds grew so large that local authorities often set up speed traps and alcohol and drug checks to maintain control.

Records had already offered the Dead a new contract when Garcia's friend Ron Rakow approached the band with a proposal: why not form their own record company?

Grateful Dead Records was officially established in April 1973. Advertising, distribution, radio promotion, and accounting staffers filled the front office. Rakow financed the band's $300,000 self-investment by selling the Dead's overseas distribution rights to Atlantic Records, a prosperous label run by Ahmet Ertegun and Jerry Wexler. Under Rakow's direction the Grateful Dead also instituted a second label, Round Records, for solo projects.

Wake of the Flood, the first Grateful Dead Records product and the first studio album since *American Beauty* in 1970, was scheduled for release later that year. The experiment in self-determination was humming along nicely. Then trouble struck.

"Shortly after our new album was released," recalled Steve Brown, the label's production and promotions director, "we discovered, much to our dismay, that sleazy counterfeit copies of *Wake of the Flood* were turning up on the East Coast." Taping concerts was one thing; but pirating the house label's first public offering was quite another. The Dead did what any robbery victim would do: they called the cops.

"I had never imagined that the Grateful Dead would end up working with the FBI," Brown recalled. "By the time the counterfeiting subsided, we had been distracted long enough to lose valuable promotion and sales momentum. Still, despite the 'evil twin' album, we were able to sell more than 400,000 copies of the real Wake, a healthy number in those days."

The Dead continued to tour. By the summer of 1973, the band had solved most of their technical problems by hauling with them a 25-ton, 26,400-watt sound system developed by Owsley's company, Alembic.

The only snag in the tour that year was not technical, but personal. Garcia and Hunter were driving to a gig in Springfield, Massachusetts, when they were pulled over for speeding in New Jersey. Garcia had no driver's license or vehicle registration. And when the trooper searched the car and found a suitcase containing drugs, Garcia was arrested. He was given a year's probation and ordered to receive addiction counseling.

Illegal drugs were by now a fact of life for Dead members. The worst offender was the anchor of the band, the one who had come to embody the spirit of the Dead in the eyes of their fans—Jerry Garcia. He was "Jerry" to Deadheads, a beloved, bearded, avuncular figure who kept the whole Grateful Dead family together.

But Garcia played the role reluctantly, loath to be anyone's role model, though it often appeared as though he had no choice. "I mean everywhere we'd go . . . it was 'Jerrr-y!! Jerrr-y!!'" said Donna Godcheaux. "And I know the effect it had on him. . . . The Dead fans put them up a lot higher than they want to be. They're just a band. They don't claim to be any more than that." Meanwhile the Deadhead flock kept multiplying; another 50,000 names were added to the band's mailing list in 1973 and 1974 alone.

The band recorded another album in March 1974 at CBS Studios in San Francisco, *The Grateful Dead from the Mars Hotel*, named after a fleabag establishment near the recording studio. The cover artwork by Mouse and Kelly—portraying a rundown hotel amid craters and rock formations on a strange, double-mooned planet—follows the title's theme. On the reverse, hotel "guests"—the band members—appear in cartoonish, space-monster incarnations, sprawled across two sofas and staring into a television in the foreground, while a spaceship sails past their hotel window. The Dead even

produced an animated television commercial to pro-
mote *Mars Hotel*.

Soon after the album's release, the Grateful Dead
decided to stop touring. Weir later explained that the
schedule had become "unmanageable":

We had pretty much roped ourselves into an unwork-
able situation. We had this huge PA that we were cart-
ing around, we had a crew of—God knows—about 40

Terrapin Station (1977)
was the Grateful Dead's
first album with Arista
Records. The Dead signed
with Arista after closing
their own recording com-
pany, Grateful Dead
Records, in 1976.

people . . . and we had to work too hard and too much to support it all. . . . It wasn't any fun after a while. . . . So we decided that we had to knock off.

Burned out by road life, members were also anxious to work on other projects, including another studio album. Garcia himself had already begun recording a second solo album. To mark the occasion, the Dead announced a "retirement party," a series of shows at Winterland Auditorium in October 1974. They planned to film the farewell performances to include in another slated project—a movie about the band—and to record the sessions for use on another live album.

Retirement proved almost as expensive as touring. The feature-length concert film, complete with animation, became so costly that Rakow had to sign over some of the band's future recordings to United Artists, another recording label, to pay production fees. Although the deal briefly eased the cash crunch, it increased the pressure to produce more—and the Dead did not like to be pressured.

Nevertheless, the Grateful Dead released the well-received *Blues for Allah*, a studio follow-up to *Mars Hotel*, in August 1975. The "retirement" concert master tapes for their live album, however, were reel-to-reel disasters—and while Lesh and Owsley sifted through them for salvageable tracks, Rakow skipped town, leaving the band to mop up a financial and creative mess. The final product, titled *Steal Your Face* to reflect Rakow's desertion, was released in 1976. It was unquestionably among the worst albums the Dead had ever produced. Even Deadheads hated it.

After only three years in business, Grateful Dead and Round Records closed down in 1976. In addition to four Grateful Dead albums, the companies had produced two albums by Robert Hunter, *Tales of the Great Rum Runners* and *Tiger Rose*; two Garcia solo albums,

Compliments of Garcia and *Reflections*; and Phil Lesh's *Seastones*, a collection of avant-garde electronic music.

In June of that year, the Dead came out of retirement to resume full-time touring. Grateful Dead members continued to involve themselves in a whirlwind of side projects during the 1970s, including a band called Kingfish—a Grateful Dead-New Riders spinoff with a honky-tonk sound—and the Good Old Boys bluegrass recording sessions, produced by Garcia.

The Grateful Dead Movie, edited by cinema buff Garcia, was released in 1977. Though it went over well with Deadheads, the general public never quite caught on. Still, the Grateful Dead—who had been cut from filmmaker Michael Wadleigh's Woodstock film and D. A. Pennebaker's Monterey Pop documentary—now had a movie all their own.

Terrapin Station, the Dead's first album on their new label, Arista Records, also came out in 1977. It is a masterpiece of orchestral wonders, in particular the title track, where strings and choral music back the band like the singing of cherubs. Garcia later explained that the title song came to him all at once: "I got that idea driving my car. I drove home real fast and sat down with the guitar and worked it all out real quick so I wouldn't forget it, because it was all there."

The album also includes a Bob Weir tune called "Estimated Prophet," a gentle poke at the more obsessive Deadheads. "It's not that one doesn't appreciate the adulation," Weir told an interviewer, "but some of the importance that people ascribe to what we're doing may be undue, it seems."

Terrapin Station is organized in the same suitelike arrangement as *Anthem of the Sun*—and it was the last of the Grateful Dead's "concept" albums. Tracks on future recordings generally would clock in at a more radio-friendly five minutes or less.

The Dead appeared on NBC TV's *Saturday Night*

Live (SNL) in September 1978 and broadcast live from Radio City Music Hall on Halloween night in a concert hosted by *SNL* regular Al Franken. In a good-natured send-up of actor Jerry Lewis's Muscular Dystrophy Telethon—Deadheads were by now calling themselves "Jerry's kids"—a solicitous Franken begged donations for a make-believe Deadhead who had injured himself trying to sneak into a show. The prize for the most generous donor? Garcia's missing finger—the Deadhead equivalent of a splinter of wood from the true cross—which Garcia supposedly kept in a box he was holding.

Jerry Garcia had always entertained the idea of traveling to Egypt, and soon after appearing on *SNL*, he fulfilled his dream: the Grateful Dead played a mystical three-night gig at the base of the floodlit Great Pyramid and within sight of the Sphinx. For band members—especially for Garcia—it was a communion of sorts, a pilgrimage to the source of their spiritual roots.

Back home in America, *Saturday Night Fever*, starring John Travolta as a disco-dancing heartbreaker, shattered box-office records and turned nightclubs like New York's Studio 57 into national shrines. The film's sound track sold millions of copies; in big-city discotheques, "night crawlers" danced until dawn to the music of the Bee Gees, Abba, the Trammps, and the "Queen of Disco," Donna Summer.

But the Grateful Dead were fadproof and rolled along at their own rock-a-bye pace. They did allow a breeze to blow through their 1978 album, *Shakedown Street*, however. Produced by Little Feat guitarist Lowell George, the title track is a funk tune with a suspiciously discolike beat and guitar riff and comes as close to fad hopping as the Dead would ever get. "I keep an open mind," Garcia told *Guitar Player* magazine. "I like disco music a lot."

Through late 1978 and 1979, while the Dead con-

tinued to tour, the Jerry Garcia Band, a solo project, released a critically acclaimed album called *Cats Under the Stars*. Bob Weir also released his second solo album, *Heaven Help the Fool*, and Mickey Hart, Bill Kreutzmann, and Phil Lesh recorded music for the 1979 Francis Ford Coppola movie *Apocalypse Now*, a nightmarish war story inspired by Joseph Conrad's "The Heart of Darkness" and starring Marlon Brando.

The Grateful Dead, meanwhile, were in trouble with their junior members, Keith and Donna Godcheaux. The demands of performing and touring together full-time while caring for Zion, their five-

The Grateful Dead in November 1978, with Keith Godcheaux on keyboards (far right) and Donna Godcheaux as vocalist (second from left). The couple would leave the Grateful Dead in February 1979, after eight years with the band.

year-old son, were affecting the couple's marriage and their relationships with other band members. The Godcheaux were drifting apart, not only from each other, but also from the rest of the band.

Finally, after performing at the "Rock for Life Benefit" at Oakland Coliseum on February 17, 1979, the Dead parted ways with the Godcheaux. Donna, at least, was relieved. "I instantly felt like about a billion pounds had been lifted from me," she told an interviewer. Her band mates had not caused the problem, she emphasized; it was instead the constant pressure to succeed:

> It's what success does to your self-image, what it does to the human spirit. It's destructive, and some people can handle it and some people can't. . . . [Y]ou're out there so long before people who adore you and [you] start to believe their image of you—or, you realize you can't live up to that image. . . . And, of course, I'm not even Jerry.

A year later, Keith Godcheaux was killed in an automobile accident. Donna Godcheaux later married a minister and moved to Petaluma, California. She never rejoined the band or sang professionally again.

Brent Mydland replaced Keith at the keyboards, debuting in April 1979 in San Jose, California. The following year marked the Dead's 15th year together, an amazingly durable act in an industry known for turnovers. While disco sputtered out and Britain invaded the United States once again—this time with the raucous, profane, teeth-gnashing "punk" sound of the Sex Pistols—the Grateful Dead cruised on.

The Grateful Dead Go to Heaven was released in 1980, with a cover featuring Dead members dressed in white suits, looking like a troupe of angels in formal wear. The band reappeared on *Saturday Night Live* to perform the sprightly "Alabama Getaway," the first single release. And for the first time in the Grateful Dead's long career, an album made *Billboard*'s Top 20.

They celebrated their anniversary by playing two shows at the University of Colorado at Boulder in June. As always, the Dead expected to spend the next decade on the road.

7 ⟩ Touch of Grey

THE GRATEFUL DEAD followed their 15th anniversary celebration with a joyous 15-show run at the Warfield Theatre in Santa Cruz, produced by Bill Graham.

In 1981 the Dead issued two live albums: *Dead Set*, a collection of touring standards, and *Dead Reckoning*, an album of acoustic or "unplugged" older songs that the band had taken on the road. Meanwhile, band members continued to produce solo albums: Bobby and the Midnights, Bob Weir's band, released a self-titled album featuring jazz drummer Billy Cobham, and in 1982 Garcia released *Run for the Roses*, a collection of original songs and covers, with his longtime Bay Area friend and musical partner, keyboardist Merl Saunders.

The Dead had no plans for a studio album during the early 1980s. They chafed at the pressure from Arista to produce more accessible and more commercial records in the tradition of *Shakedown Street* and *The Grateful Dead Go to Heaven*. Instead, they completed a succession of concert tours and side projects. But the band's dogged touring endeared them to fans, who regularly filled stadium-sized concert halls.

By the 1980s, the Grateful Dead had launched a cottage industry of books, magazines, radio programs, and merchandise for fans, and they had appeared on *Saturday Night Live*. Many products, such as this 1990 book *Grateful Dead Family Album*, still incorporated artist Stanley Mouse's variations on his 1966 skull and roses motif.

By now the Grateful Dead was no longer merely a band; it was a musical phenomenon, an industry of its own, with books, monthly magazines, a syndicated radio program, and a catalog of merchandise, all available to fans. The Dead still loved to play extended live jams and continued to push boundaries, developing two wide-open musical segments in each performance that they called "drums" and "space," in which they melded jazz and rock into wild and ecstatic improvisational trips. Sometimes, Garcia would say, when everything was just right, "the music play[ed] the band."

Despite the vast popularity of the band's live performances, some critics speculated that the Dead were missing out on an even broader audience or might simply play themselves out in a shrinking circle of fans, while rock music evolved around them. "By largely forswearing studio albums after the 1970s," one rock journalist noted, "the Dead lost the interest of much of the mainstream and important cutting-edge pop audiences of the last two decades."

Harsher critics accused the group of peddling memories to a willing and sentimental public, labeling the Grateful Dead a cover band who imitated a younger version of itself. The Dead were "nostalgia mongers," remarked one observer, "offering facile reminiscence to an audience with no memory of its own."

And during the early 1980s, even some of the group's most loyal supporters began wondering how and why the Dead carried on. Band members often seemed unenthusiastic during performances, appearing to many as though they were sleepwalking through sets. Garcia in particular was becoming a listless and error-prone guitarist, singing with a shadow of his usual joy and passion and looking worn and overweight.

Rumors about Garcia's health and about the cause of his faltering performances began spreading among Deadheads, who generally attributed the change to drug use. One fan at a 1983 show wondered aloud, "I wanna know if . . . Jerry really does heroin. . . . And I'd like to know when the last time [band members] did acid was, because a lot of their audience still does it."

The Grateful Dead insisted that they did not encourage drug use. "We're not selling drugs or promoting drugs," Garcia told an interviewer in 1980. "The fact that we all take drugs isn't even true. And nobody takes drugs regularly." But by the mid-1980s, Garcia could no longer truthfully make such a statement. He himself was using cocaine and heroin, and he "got so trashed out for the last few years that he just wasn't really playing," sound engineer Dan Healey told *People Weekly* in 1995.

Band members stayed involved in outside projects during this time. Garcia wrote the score for a reprise of TV's the *Twilight Zone*. And in 1984, under his direction, the Grateful Dead established and funded the Rex Foundation, a nonprofit charity named after road manager Donald "Rex" Jackson, which gave grants to needy causes and individuals, from at-risk youngsters to struggling composers. But the Dead's attempt to record an album that year petered out after two aimless weeks in the studio. "We had the tunes," keyboardist Brent Mydland remembered, "but there was no real drive to go in and record."

Meanwhile, Garcia's drug addiction intensified. He had started out as a young man using LSD in a search for expanded consciousness; now all he wanted was the next fix. His band mates were aware of the problem. In fact, they took the huge risk of telling Garcia to clean up or leave the band. Jerry's survival—and his health— meant more to them than the band did. He was no good to them dead.

Garcia promised to seek help. But on January 18, 1985, a policeman patrolling Golden Gate Park found him freebasing cocaine in the front seat of a parked car and discovered 23 packages of heroin and cocaine in a suitcase in the car. The judge on Garcia's case spared him imprisonment and ordered him into an addiction treatment program. Garcia later admitted that he had been using heroin for eight years—but he described it as an occasional thing, a way "to distance myself a little from the world."

In the summer of 1986, the newly clean Garcia led the Grateful Dead in another tour. Rockers Tom Petty and Bob Dylan traveled with them—and the star accompaniment seemed to revitalize the band. But one evening shortly after the tour ended, an exhausted Garcia collapsed in his San Rafael home and slipped into a diabetic coma. His body had finally succumbed to physical abuse.

When Garcia emerged from the coma several days later, he learned that the seizure had disrupted his memory and his coordination. He had lost his ability to play guitar. For the next three months, with the help of Merl Saunders, Garcia painstakingly relearned the instrument. The good wishes and gifts of Deadheads encouraged him as well: "The fans put life into me," he later said.

By 1987 Garcia had fully recovered, and the Grateful Dead released *In the Dark*, their first nonlive recording in seven years. The first single, "Touch of Grey," set Garcia's twangy guitar to a rolling, up-tempo riff and an upbeat refrain: "We will get by/We will survive." The song achieved what no Grateful Dead single had ever done: it broke into the *Billboard* Top 10, pushing *In the Dark* sales into the stratosphere, higher on the album charts than any previous Dead project.

In a striking "Touch of Grey" video that played off the band's longtime motif, members of the Dead appear on a spotlit stage as a band of clothed skeletons. At one point a bothersome dog grabs a leg bone right out from under one skeleton and takes off with it.

A scene from the Grateful Dead's whimsical 1987 "Touch of Grey" video, in which band members appear as clothed skeletons.

The Dead had taken only 22 years to create a hit.

"Touch of Grey" spawned a whole legion of new Grateful Dead fans who were younger than the actual band. The post-baby boom generation began "turning on and tuning in" to the San Francisco sound that had peaked when most of them were toddlers.

In a slightly disdainful nod to these newcomers,

Jerry Garcia sends New Year greetings to fans in this 1986 photograph. After surviving a seizure and diabetic coma earlier in the year, Garcia had to relearn how to play the guitar. He was fully recovered by 1987.

longtime Deadheads began referring to them as "Touch Heads." Hunter remembered being accosted by one longtime fan after finishing a radio interview one day. "Hey!" the guy bellowed at the lyricist. "I heard on your interview there that you were writing some new tunes with Garcia. I sure hope you guys aren't making a record, because you're already popular enough, and I'm having enough trouble with the new fans."

The sentiment seemed common among traditional

Deadheads, some of whom grumbled that "their" band had sold out. Though the Dead enjoyed their newfound success, they rejected such criticism as uninformed. "We're not going to set out to make a hit record," Hunter maintained. "We didn't set out to make one this time. It's just the coincidence—this tune seemed to click with some emergent factor in American consciousness, and blammo, there it was. The shoe fit this time."

The tellingly titled *Built to Last* album followed *In the Dark* in 1989, yielding the advice-laden hit single "Foolish Heart." In an interview late that year, Garcia and Weir joked that the song's lyrics were oddly cautionary coming from a band known for wild excess. Garcia recalled,

> When Hunter and I were working on this tune, I said, "This is an advice song!" I mean, the lyrics are "Never give your love, my friend/to a foolish heart." Is that really good advice? Is that what we want to say? Shouldn't we tell them, "Hey, brush your teeth twice a day!"

"It was Jerry at his avuncular best," Weir remarked. "This is our Dutch uncle tune."

But in Garcia's own life, the lessons of "Foolish Heart" had not come easily. His marriage to "Mountain Girl" Carolyn Adams, the Merry Prankster of his Haight-Ashbury days, ended in divorce—the second for Garcia—when Adams learned that he had fathered a child with another woman. The two already had two children of their own; Garcia now had four daughters of three different mothers.

The Grateful Dead outlived the vinyl age of recording, beginning the 1990s with the live double compact disc *Without a Net*, their eighth release on the Arista label. In 1990 the Dead became America's "longest-running" rock and roll show, celebrating their 25th year as a band.

They were the sole survivors of the Haight-Ashbury era. Even the Jefferson Starship, now barely recognizable as the former Jefferson Airplane, had delivered its last album in 1989 before disbanding. Like the song "Touch of Grey" had promised, the Dead were getting by.

But the new decade brought tragedy as well. In 1990 Grateful Dead keyboard player and backup singer Brent Mydland died of a drug overdose, the third Dead member, current or former, to die. Until they found a permanent replacement for Mydland, the band tapped keyboardist Bruce Hornsby, a friend of the band with a successful career of his own.

The same year, the Dead hired a video specialist to create concert visuals. Using computerized technology, the artist perched behind a console in the band's sound tower like a radar man onboard a ship, directing wild, amoebic swirls of light, mandala patterns, and psychedelically altered videos of the band across two giant onstage screens. The effect was reminiscent of the Trips Festival light-and-pigment shows—updated for the '90s and enhanced with digital power.

True to their hippie roots, the Dead often invited visiting musicians on stage to jam. In March 1990 at New York's Nassau Coliseum, for example, the acclaimed saxophonist Branford Marsalis joined the Grateful Dead. A reviewer later described the session:

> The band began the simple, undulating melody of a 1971 Garcia tune called "Birdsong," and the guitarist started to play genial host to the jazzman. Smiling above his white beard, Garcia danced a little shuffle, guided Marsalis through the changes, and gave him some room to play. Soon Marsalis's soprano sax and Garcia's bell-like guitar were somersaulting through

the upper reaches of the audible spectrum—trading licks, chiming together—while Lesh's bass lines bounded around in the depths. The entire band seemed galvanized by Marsalis's presence, and the crowd—even those who had, like, no idea who the dude with the horn was—settled down for a night of exploration.

Lesh, Weir, Kreutzmann, and Garcia in the video for "Throwing Stones," a single from the album *In the Dark* (1987).

The Dead opened the new decade with one of the highest-grossing tours in the industry, outpacing even hugely popular stadium bands such as U2, Pink Floyd, and the Rolling Stones. Beginning in 1989, they appeared for six years on *Forbes* magazine's annual list of the world's most highly paid entertainers, in the com-

95

With their first *Billboard* Top 10 hit, "Touch of Grey," the Grateful Dead drew legions of new fans, many of whom were younger than the band itself. Longtime followers began referring to more recent fans as "Touch Heads."

pany of Michael Jackson, Madonna, ex–Beatle Paul McCartney, and the Stones. Ticket sales climbed: the Dead passed the $10-, $20-, and $30-million mark in yearly concert receipts.

And the Deadheads' thousand-wheeled caravan trundled on, turning stadiums and arenas into little Woodstock nations everywhere the band toured. A daylight walk through the parking lot of a Dead venue was like a trip through a gypsy campground: Deadheads would spread out, settle in, and set up shop across acres of asphalt at each tour stop, establishing temporary communities sustained by the sale and barter of food, clothing, jewelry, and artwork. Whole families—preschoolers included—lounged beside weather-beaten vans and trailers and near jewelry and clothing stands under flimsy sunshades.

Deadheads were walking displays of each other's tie-dyed and handmade clothing. Some wore temporary tattoos of skulls and roses or of multicolored dancing bears, another Dead emblem; others sported T-shirts reading "Europe '72" or "Mean People Suck." Teenagers in baggy clothes and stringy hair clustered in circles to play Hackysack—an unofficial Deadhead game in which a small beanbag must be tossed to other players using no hands.

Dead music and marijuana smoke would issue from dozens of parked vehicles; walking past cars was like surfing an all-Dead radio band. A discreetly conducted drug trade would take place out of view, its effects evident in many "useless smiles"—Deadspeak for those tripping on LSD.

Many caravaners slept in their cars—radios blaring and sneaker-clad feet dangling out of windows—as they waited for sunset and the next concert to begin. When the Dead finished a two- or three-day gig, the city in the parking lot came down—and went up again at the next tour stop.

With increased commercial success came more tragedy for the Grateful Dead. On October 25, 1991, a helicopter flying Bill Graham and his fiancée to his northern California home crashed into an electrical tower during a pounding rainstorm. The pilot and both passengers were killed.

Graham's death at age 60 devastated band members; the Dead owed much of their early success to the promoter's tireless work. In a daylong concert tribute to Graham in Golden Gate Park, the Grateful Dead drew a crowd of 500,000—similar in size to that of Woodstock.

The band had just entered another record-breaking year in 1992 when Jerry Garcia collapsed in his San Rafael home following his own mini-tour with the Jerry Garcia Band. The "official" cause of Garcia's illness was exhaustion brought on by a poor diet and lack of exercise. Grateful Dead spokesman Dennis McNally strongly denied persistent rumors that Garcia was using drugs again. "He's never listened to other people about his health," McNally told *Rolling Stone* magazine. "But it appears that he is listening to the message of his body, which is telling him: 'Time to clean up your act. Time to knock off the chili dogs and milkshakes and all that stuff.'"

Determined to recover, Garcia dieted and lost 60 pounds, vowed to quit smoking, and hired a personal fitness trainer. The Dead resumed traveling in early 1993, having canceled a tour that had grossed $26 million between January and August of 1992. At the first gig in Denver, a visibly happy and slimmer Garcia called this period "the Golden Age of the Grateful Dead."

In subsequent interviews, Garcia would avoid discussing his illness, and he took pains to reassure fans that he was doing well. "This is the best I've felt in years," he told *Rolling Stone*. Garcia half joked that the enforced break from touring "was good for all of us. Right now we're happening. We're enjoying what we're doing. It's all new again."

But Garcia knew that he had truly come close to dying. "I think it's helpful to have those kinds of near-death experiences once in a while," he said. "They kind of brighten up your perspective." The episode, he said, may have caused him finally to take notice of the way he was treating himself:

> In a way I was lucky, insofar as I had an iron constitution. But time naturally gets to you, and finally your body just doesn't spring back the way it did. I think it had to get as bad as it did before I would get serious about it. I mean, it's a powerful incentive, the possibility that, hey, if you keep going the way you are, in two years you're going to be dead.

After years without an album release, the Grateful Dead again planned a studio session for the summer of 1993. "I hope it turns out even halfway decent," Garcia mused in his characteristic self-deprecating way. "When we first started making records, I used to have ideas. Now I see our records as a long string of failures. I see it in terms of near misses."

8 One More Saturday Night

THE SAN FRANCISCO HIPPIES of the Grateful Dead emerged from the "roaring '80s" so conspicuously wealthy that a younger Garcia might have accused his older self of selling out. But somehow the Dead were able to reconcile the conflict between their early ideals and their current success. They may have been doing big business, but they did so with bohemian flair.

Grateful Dead Productions now occupied a sprawling Victorian house—similar to 710 Ashbury—in San Rafael, with 50 to 60 full-time employees, including an archivist whose sole job was to maintain concert tapes. Grateful Dead company employees received health benefits and bonuses and were included in a company profit-sharing plan. The company pulled down more than $40 million in ticket and merchandise sales through the Grateful Dead Mercantile Company in 1993, and the concert industry magazine *Pollstar* had named the band North America's top-grossing act for two years running.

The band and their "Deadquarters" were the subject of an admiring 1994 profile in the glossy business magazine *Inc.*: "Whether or not they think of themselves as entrepreneurs," the magazine declared, "the mem-

Jerry Garcia performs in Pittsburgh on June 30, 1995, less than two months before his death.

bers of the Grateful Dead have what owners of other growing businesses strive for: an organization that thrives but doesn't distract [from its product]."

Meanwhile, Jerry Garcia had become a franchise of his own. Drawing on his early art training, Garcia produced paintings for a nationwide touring exhibition; some of his works fetched as much as $20,000 each. He designed wet suits for scuba divers and limited-edition watches for fans. A suite was named after him at the Los Angeles Prescott Hotel, where selections of his art were displayed. But perhaps the most ironic Garcia product was his line of arty, colorful "J. Garcia" neckties designed for retail clothing outlets. "He never wore a tie in his life," one Deadhead marveled.

Garcia's name and face also had become commodities. As a nostalgic symbol of an aging generation, Garcia was instantly identifiable to his fellow baby boomers in his radio advertisement for San Francisco-based Levi Jeans and in the fruity "Cherry Garcia" flavor launched by the Vermont Deadhead owners of Ben and Jerry's Ice Cream.

But the hippie spirit had not died. Both Garcia and the Grateful Dead were eager to share their wealth with less fortunate people. Garcia himself believed that the band's success was due largely to incredible good luck: "We've been falling uphill for 27 years," he wryly noted. So he gave money to causes like the Haight-Ashbury Free Clinic, a health-care and drug treatment center for the poor and one of the last surviving institutions of the neighborhood's heyday. And the Grateful Dead's Rex Foundation was now distributing $1 million annually in grants.

Meanwhile, the legions of Dead fans numbered 100,000 in the United States and 20,000 abroad—and had penetrated cyberspace. A computer user "surfing" the Internet would encounter scores of World Wide Web pages authored by Dead Freaks for sharing news, conversation, Dead-inspired on-line artwork, and even a Deadhead cookbook and Deadhead dictionary. (When Garcia forgot a lyric on stage, fans called it a "Jerry gap." A concert parking lot filled with vendors was called "Shakedown Street" and yuppie fans were "Shakers." A "Jerryiott" was a hotel where band members stayed while on tour.)

The logistics of touring grew increasingly complicated—and difficult—as the band's popularity rose. Some local jurisdictions began banning Grateful Dead gigs in their communities. Parents frequently accused the band of tacitly encouraging their fans to leave their homes and join the groupie caravan, which included scores of teenage runaways. For their part, Deadheads largely saw themselves as a caring and tightly knit family.

But for all the warmth and protection fans felt as part of the Deadhead "family," hugely popular Grateful Dead concerts were not always safe. In an episode eerily reminiscent of the Altamont tragedy, a young fan was beaten to death outside a show at Brendan Byrne Arena in New Jersey in 1994. Though Deadheads blamed stadium security, the guards denied any involvement in the beating.

There were other dangers as well. Drug use was long thought a harmless—and for many, an essential—part of the Dead experience. But drug taking, always hazardous, was now fraught with new risks. Many new drugs and street versions of older drugs were purer and more potent than ever—some were even life-threatening. Moreover, with the surge in drug-related crime in U.S. cities, the federal government passed measures for stricter punishments, assigning "mandatory minimum" prison sentences even for first-time offenders.

Frequently the targets of local police because drug use was popular among them, Deadheads often felt the brunt of the crackdowns. And rumors spread about an

"Operation Dead End" investigation run by the federal Drug Enforcement Agency (DEA) and aimed specifically at Dead fans (the DEA denied its existence). Nonetheless, by spring of 1994, an estimated 2,000 Deadheads—most in their late teens and 20s—were imprisoned for concert-related drug offenses.

At the heart of the controversy was the Grateful Dead, caught between the law and parents' concerns and the "image" their fans had of them. In a *New Republic* article on March 21, 1994, Frank Smyth accused the Grateful Dead of "trying to deny [their] own association with drugs" and chastised the band for not mounting an all-out challenge to mandatory minimum sentencing. Band members did touch on the subject of imprisoned Deadheads in their 1993 speech upon being inducted into the Rock and Roll Hall of Fame, and the Rex Foundation donated $10,000 to Families Against Mandatory Minimums. But Smyth called the gift "pocket change" in light of the Grateful Dead's vast army of fans and their own enormous concert profits. "The Grateful Dead were pioneers with LSD in the '60s," Smyth wrote. "But you wouldn't know that from what band members say now."

The band responded not by defending drug use but by reminding fans that the Dead operated in a different world now. "The band feels horrible about being used as a Judas goat—a band that gathers people together to give the police an easy opportunity to make arrests," Dennis McNally told *Rolling Stone* magazine. "But by now, most Deadheads have gotten the message that you can't do illegal drugs in our parking lot and expect to stay to see the show. There may be a never-never land, but it ain't the Grateful Dead parking lot."

In fact, lyricist Robert Hunter had commented similarly on the fantasy of a Deadhead fairyland in 1988:

[The] Grateful Dead have become, by their very size, a microcosmic example of what's happened in the world at large. Some of you are going to get killed. Some are going to get run over, some of you are going to get your arms broken, and some of you are going to fry your heads out from being dosed [with LSD], and short of authoritarian control . . . what [are] you gonna do? You can pay your money, you can take your chances. But be aware, you know. Be aware. Don't come to a Grateful Dead concert feeling that you're just going to melt into the mix and providence is all going to take care of you. Like that. You must be a responsible human being.

As Grateful Dead merchandising grew, Jerry Garcia became an industry of his own. Here he displays a number of his original paintings, which were included in a nationwide touring exhibition of his artwork.

For all their public declarations against irresponsible drug use, the Grateful Dead still sometimes sent mixed messages to fans. Garcia, for example—"Captain Trips" of earlier times—spoke glowingly more than once of his experiences with psychedelic drugs. "Psychedelics are

A throng of Grateful Dead fans during the band's 1995 anniversary tour. Less than a month after this concert, Jerry Garcia checked into the Betty Ford Center for a drug treatment program.

still the most important thing that ever happened to me," he told one interviewer. "Psychedelics is a lot of why I'm here and doing what I'm doing. And a lot of the vision I have—such as it is—I owe to my psychedelic experience. Nothing has opened me up like psychedelics did." For Dead fans who virtually worshipped Garcia, this kind of talk was tantamount to an endorsement of drug use.

Despite such troubles, the group's 1993-94 tour was highly successful—and life was good for Garcia. He married his girlfriend, Deborah Koons, on Valentine's Day, 1994, and had begun spending more time with his daughters, whom he felt he had previously neglected. "They've been very patient with me," he said.

In 1995 the Grateful Dead turned 30. Only the

Kinks and the Rolling Stones had survived longer. The anniversary tour became a traveling celebration of the endless romance between the Dead and their fans. Ticket demands quickly outstripped the supply. In city after city, fans stood optimistically outside concert halls with index fingers held up—the traditional Deadhead signal of someone in need of "a miracle," that one ticket or free pass to the show.

But the chronic ticket crunch began to breed tension among the haves and have-nots. Two weeks after the Dead's June anniversary concert, a fan melee in Albany, New York, ended in 50 arrests. A month later, police in Noblesville, Indiana, squared off against a rock- and bottle-throwing crowd of ticketless fans. Dozens were arrested and several people, including four police officers, were injured. Fearing further violence, the Dead canceled their performance for the first time since Altamont.

In explaining the cancellation, Grateful Dead Productions posted a blunt statement on the Internet. "If you don't have a ticket," it read, "don't come." The letter also warned fans that further gate-crashing might force the Dead to cease touring entirely. The tone might have stunned anyone who knew the band during mellower times. But the Grateful Dead ran a business now and could not risk further antagonizing the communities that hosted concerts.

Even Mother Nature did not smile upon the anniversary tour. Three fans outside a concert in Washington, D.C., were struck by lightning. A few days later, a makeshift porch at a Dead campsite near St. Louis, Missouri, collapsed, injuring more than 100 fans. People began wondering if the band was cursed. But the Dead dismissed that idea. "I don't regard this as a test of karma," McNally insisted.

But Garcia, at least, was once again battling his own demon of drug addiction—and losing. Soon after a concert at Chicago's Soldier Field on July 9, 1995, Garcia left work on a new album and checked into the Betty Ford Center, a drug treatment facility in Rancho Mirage, California. He was determined to be clean in time for the Dead's fall tour, and he was planning to give away his oldest daughter, Heather, at her upcoming wedding.

Though Garcia left the clinic two weeks ahead of schedule and without formally completing the program to spend his 53rd birthday at home with his family, he would enter another program soon afterward. Deborah Garcia recalled in *Rolling Stone* magazine,

> Jerry came out [of Betty Ford], and he looked just great. He'd lost weight, and he was smiling. He was doing really well, and he was strong. He was clean.... he wanted to come home. So I said, "You can come home if you continue in the recovery stuff." And he wanted to do that because he was feeling good about himself. He was facing his pain and his joy in a real way.

He checked into Serenity Knolls, a rehabilitation facility closer to his Marin County home.

Sometime before dawn on Wednesday, August 9, Jerry Garcia's heart stopped. Paramedics summoned to Serenity Knolls were unable to revive him, and he was pronounced dead that morning.

Deborah Garcia later told friends that Jerry had died with a smile on his lips. The long, strange trip was over. Garcia left behind four daughters: Heather, 32; Annabelle, 25; Teresa, 21; and Keelin, 7.

At sunrise on August 9, the news was released. Word of Garcia's death spread rapidly through news wires and radio and television broadcasts into homes and offices in thousands of cities and towns. Scores of fans logged onto computer networks to post their condolences and share Grateful Dead memories. The Deadhead cyber-board called "The Well" was so overwhelmed that the whole system eventually crashed. Jerry had turned the Internet into a wailing wall.

One by one, Garcia's friends and band mates also learned the news. Bob Weir was on his way to a solo show at the Casino Ballroom in Hampton Beach, New Hampshire, when he heard of his friend's death. He decided to perform as planned that night and dedicated the concert to Garcia. "If our dear departed friend proved anything to us," he told his audience, "he proved that great music can make sad times better."

Around the country, Jerry's mourners spontaneously gathered, carrying candles, flowers, and pictures of the beloved musician. At Strawberry Fields in Manhattan's Central Park, on the steps of the Lincoln Memorial in Washington, in Houston's Tranquility Park, on Independence Mall in Philadelphia, and in San Francisco, outside 710 Ashbury Street and in Golden Gate Park, strangers hugged and cried and sang Grateful Dead songs.

One U.S. senator, Patrick Leahy of Vermont, even called a press conference to share his sorrow. Leahy told reporters that he once escorted Garcia around Congress and introduced him to several politicians, including Senator Strom Thurmond, a South Carolina Republican and the oldest man in the Senate. "I understand you're a rock star, boy," the nonagenarian Thurmond drawled. "I do my best," replied the embarrassed musician.

Garcia's death made the front pages of nearly every major American newspaper, including the *New York Times*, the *Washington Post*, the *Los Angeles Times*, the *Chicago Tribune*, and the *San Francisco Chronicle* and *Herald-Examiner*. "A Rock-and-Roll Patriarch Dies," declared the front-page headline of the *Philadelphia Inquirer*.

Tributes to the leader of the Dead family took

many forms, from the utterly bizarre—the National Space Society in Washington announced plans to "place the remains of Mr. Garcia in eternal earth orbit" (this did not happen)—to the nostalgic—LSD guru Timothy Leary, then 74, urged grieving fans to "Hang on, hang in, and hang out." Sales of Dead albums skyrocketed; department stores ran out of "J. Garcia" ties.

The reaction to Garcia's death was so strong and the outpouring so great that it often seemed impossible to put into words. "There's not a sentence in the world that would respectably justify the life and music of Jerry Garcia," Branford Marsalis said upon hearing the news. Bob Dylan, a legend in his own right, related similar sentiments:

> To me he wasn't only a musician and friend, he was more like a big brother who taught me more than he'll ever know. . . . His playing was moody, awesome, sophisticated, hypnotic, and subtle. There's no way to convey the loss. It just digs down really deep.

More than 200 mourners attended a private funeral on Friday, August 11, at St. Stephen's Episcopal Church in Belvedere, California. (The apparent allusion to the Grateful Dead song "St. Stephen" was reportedly a coincidence.) Mourners from all over the country and from all parts of Garcia's life attended: Bob Weir, Phil Lesh, Mickey Hart, Bill Kreutzmann, and Vince Welnick, the Dead's newest keyboardist. Ex-member Donna Godcheaux was there, as were Bob Dylan and Ken Kesey. Lyricist Robert Hunter read a poem he composed in honor of his friend, asking "Now that the singer is gone/Where shall I go for the song?"

Two days later, 25,000 people joined surviving band members for a public memorial service in Golden Gate Park, one of Garcia's favorite haunts. The Dead tribe had gathered once more in all its glorious color and fellow-

ship, standing among bouquets and burning incense, listening to Garcia's friends tell stories. Drum circles pounded out laments, and Dead music drifted through the bay air.

Deadheads consoled themselves with the knowledge that their 9 1/2-fingered guitarist had lived a full and extraordinary life. But he'd also lived under the tremendous pressure of conforming to an image his fans had of him: "Jerry," their Buddha, mentor, messiah, and family friend. Garcia had seen fans' adoration on T-shirts and bumper stickers that read "Jerry Saves." He'd heard it in Deadhead cries of "Jerrr-y!" during performances. He had reached the point where he would say almost nothing during concerts, fearing that his words were

An impromptu gathering of Grateful Dead fans at the corner of San Francisco's Haight and Ashbury Streets on August 10, 1995, mourning the death of Jerry Garcia.

taken too seriously by fans who seemed to believe in him more than they did in themselves. He had never wanted such power; managing his own life had been difficult enough.

"Initially, when we started the Grateful Dead," Garcia had said in 1972, "we didn't have anything goin' anyway. We were nowhere, but it was groovy." He went on:

> That "nowhere" state is a thing that everybody can revert to and be cool behind. So we're not losin' or gainin' anything, we're just goin' through the changes. And the changes have brought us this far, and showed us this much, and they're continuing to take us along. That's the ride we're on.

The ride had carried Garcia and the Grateful Dead so far afield that "nowhere" would never be reclaimed. They had become so important to so many people that they would never be permitted to slip back into obscurity.

Though Grateful Dead Productions laid off several employees after Garcia's death, it made no announcement regarding the future of the band. The Grateful Dead did release *Hundred Year Hall*, an album of live sessions from the Germany leg of the Europe '72 tour featuring some of Pigpen's last performances. The album quickly hit *Billboard's* Top 40.

But though rumors persisted about a Grateful Dead tribute tour of surviving band members, many people could not imagine the band carrying on. "[A]s an institution, the Dead may turn out to be as fragile as one man's health," *New York Times* pop critic Jon Pareles wrote. Though "Uncle John's Band" had survived death, burnout, bad luck, controversy, music fads, and the ever-shortening American attention span, it appeared that it would not survive Garcia himself. "Jerry Garcia *was* the

Grateful Dead," said one fan, "so it's hard to see the band without him."

The Grateful Dead had lasted for three decades, released scores of albums, and played thousands of concerts, no two the same. As a work in progress, the tours would be forever left incomplete by Garcia's death.

But interesting things had happened along the way. The Grateful Dead had created a world within a world, a microcosm with its own customs, currency, language, dress, and movable landscape. In a society addicted to violence, they had sought peace. In a "disposable" culture, Deadheads wanted a lasting world. The Grateful Dead's music, and the collective memories stored in the hearts—and home tapes—of countless Deadheads, will no doubt continue to preserve that world long after its deities have disappeared.

Grateful Dead (1967)

Anthem of the Sun (1968)

Aoxomoxoa (1969)

Live Dead (1970)

Workingman's Dead (1970)

American Beauty (1970)

The Grateful Dead (1971)

Europe '72 (1972)

History of the Grateful Dead, Volume 1: Bear's Choice (1973)

Wake of the Flood (1973)

Best of the Grateful Dead: Skeletons from the Closet (1974)

The Grateful Dead from the Mars Hotel (1974)

Blues for Allah (1975)

Steal Your Face (1976)

Terrapin Station (1977)

What a Long, Strange Trip It's Been (1977)

Shakedown Street (1978)

The Grateful Dead Go to Heaven (1980)

Dead Reckoning (1981)

Dead Set (1981)

In the Dark (1987)

Built to Last (1989)

Without a Net (1990)

Deadicated (1991)

Hundred Year Hall (1995)

Chronology ★ ★ ★ ★ ★ ★ ★ ★ ★ ★ ★ ★ ★ ★ ★ ★

1942   Jerome John "Jerry" Garcia is born August 1 in San Francisco

1957   Jerry Garcia gets his first guitar

1960   Garcia is dishonorably discharged from the U.S. Army after serving nine months; meets future songwriting partner Robert Hunter

1961   Phil Lesh meets Jerry Garcia during Garcia's solo banjo performance on "The Midnight Special," a San Francisco radio program

1964   Garcia forms the acoustic band Mother McCree's Uptown Jug Champions, with guitarists Bob Weir and David Nelson and vocalist and harmonica player Ron "Pigpen" McKernan

1965   Mother McCree's becomes the blues-rock electric band the Warlocks, with Garcia, Weir, McKernan, Lesh, and Bill Kreutzmann

        The Warlocks change their name to the Grateful Dead

1966   The Grateful Dead perform at the Trips Festival in San Francisco, January 21-22

        The Grateful Dead sign a recording contract with Warner Bros.

        Band members return to 710 Ashbury Street, in the Haight-Ashbury district of San Francisco

        LSD is declared illegal by the federal government

1967   The Dead perform before 20,000 people at the Human Be-In at Golden Gate Park, San Francisco, in January

        Their first album, *Grateful Dead*, is released in March

        The Dead perform at the Monterey Pop Festival in June before a crowd of 90,000

        Two band members are arrested for drug possession in a police raid on 710 Ashbury

1969   The Grateful Dead play the Woodstock Music and Arts Festival in August

The band refuses to go onstage during a violence-marred concert at the Altamont Speedway near San Francisco in December

1970   *Live Dead, Workingman's Dead*, and *American Beauty* are released

1971   Keyboardist Keith Godcheaux joins the Grateful Dead

1972   The Dead tour Europe; a three-album set of live recordings from the tour, *Europe '72*, is released

Donna Godcheaux, vocalist and wife of Keith Godcheaux, joins the band

1973   "Pigpen" McKernan dies of liver failure

1978   The Grateful Dead play for three days in Egypt in September

1980   The band releases its 12th studio album, *The Grateful Dead Go To Heaven*

1985   Garcia is arrested for drug possession in January; he is ordered into a drug rehabilitation program

The band celebrates its 20th anniversary in June

1987   *In the Dark* becomes the Grateful Dead's best-selling album

1989   *Forbes* magazine lists the Grateful Dead among top-grossing U.S. entertainers; the band remains on the list in 1990

1992   Garcia collapses from exhaustion; the band cancels remaining tour dates

1993   The Grateful Dead are inducted into the Rock 'n' Roll Hall of Fame

1995   Garcia dies of a heart attack on August 9 in a Marin County, California, drug rehabilitation center

25,000 people join surviving Grateful Dead members at an official memorial service for Garcia in Golden Gate Park on August 11

Further Reading ★ ★ ★ ★ ★ ★ ★ ★ ★ ★ ★ ★ ★

DeCurtis, Anthony. "The Music Never Stops: The *Rolling Stone* Interview with Jerry Garcia." *Rolling Stone*, 2 September 1993.

Foege, Alec. "Funeral for a Friend." *Rolling Stone*, 21 September 1995.

Gans, David. *Conversations with the Dead*. New York: Citadel Underground, 1993.

Gans, David, and Peter Simon. *Playing in the Band*. New York: St. Martin's Press, 1985.

Gilmore, Mikal. "Jerry Garcia, 1942-1995." *Rolling Stone*, 21 September 1995.

Goldberg, Michael. "Garcia, Truckin' Again." *Rolling Stone*, 21 January 1993.

Harrison, Hank. *The Dead, Vol. 1: A Social History of the Haight-Ashbury Experience*. San Francisco: The Archives Press, 1972.

Jackson, Blair. *Goin' Down the Road: A Grateful Dead Traveling Companion*. New York: Harmony Books, 1992.

Mouse, Stanley. *Freehand: The Art of Stanley Mouse*. Berkeley-Hong-Kong: SLG Books, 1993.

Perry, Charles. *The Haight-Ashbury: A History*. New York: Vintage Books, 1985.

Troy, Sandy. *Captain Trips: A Biography of Jerry Garcia*. New York: Thunder's Mouth Press, 1994.

————. *One More Saturday Night: Reflections with the Grateful Dead, Dead Family and Dead Heads*. New York: St. Martin's Press, 1991.

Sean Piccoli covers culture and politics for the *Washington Times* in Washington, D.C., and is the author of a Chelsea House biography of Jimi Hendrix. He earned a B.A. in journalism from the University of Wisconsin in Madison. Piccoli has attended only one Grateful Dead concert.

Leeza Gibbons is a reporter for and cohost of the nationally syndicated television program *Entertainment Tonight* and NBC's daily talk show *Leeza*. A graduate of the University of South Carolina's School of Journalism, Gibbons joined the on-air staff of *Entertainment Tonight* in 1984 after cohosting WCBS-TV's *Two on the Town* in New York City. Prior to that, she cohosted *PM Magazine* on WFAA-TV in Dallas, Texas, and on KFDM-TV in Beaumont, Texas. Gibbons also hosts the annual Miss Universe, Miss U.S.A., and Miss Teen U.S.A. pageants, as well as the annual Hollywood Christmas Parade. She is active in a number of charities and has served as the national chairperson for the Spinal Muscular Atrophy Division of the Muscular Dystrophy Association; each September, Gibbons cohosts the National MDA Telethon with Jerry Lewis.

Picture Credits ★ ★ ★ ★ ★ ★ ★ ★ ★ ★ ★ ★ ★ ★ ★ ★

page

2: pen & ink by Mouse/ Kelley, © 1966	42: photo by Gene Anthony	76: UPI/Corbis-Bettmann
10: Archive Photos	46: photo by Gene Anthony	79: acrylic by Mouse/Kelley, © 1976
13: Archive Photos/Frank Driggs Collection	51: photo by Gene Anthony	83: photo by Jay Blakesberg
16: UPI/Corbis-Bettmann	52: Archive Photos/Tucker Ranson	86: gouache by Stanley Mouse, © 1990
18: photo by Herb Greene	55: UPI/Bettmann	91: photo by Jay Blakesberg
23: Archive Photos	58: Photofest	92: photo by Jay Blakesberg
26: Archive Photos	63: Archive Photos	94-95: photo by Jay Blakesberg
29: Archive Photos	64: UPI/Corbis-Bettmann	100: AP/Wide World Photos
32: photo by Gene Anthony	67: airbrush by Mouse/Kelley, © 1972	105: photo by Jay Blakesberg
37: photo by Gene Anthony	70: photo by Gene Anthony	106: AP/Wide World Photos
38: photo by Gene Anthony	72: airbrush by Mouse/Kelley, © 1974	111: UPI/Corbis-Bettmann
41: photo by Gene Anthony		